EARTH
POWER

About the Author

Scott Cunningham was born in Royal Oak, Michigan, on June 27, 1956. He learned about Wicca while still in high school and practiced elemental magic for twenty years. He experienced, researched, then wrote about what he learned in his magical training. Scott is credited with writing more than thirty books (both fiction and nonfiction). He passed from this incarnation on March 28, 1993, but his work and his words live on.

EARtH
POweR

techniques of natural magic

S c o t t C u n n i n g h a m

Llewellyn Publications
Woodbury, Minnesota

REVISED EDITION
Third Printing, 2008
First edition, thirty-two printings

Book design and layout by Joanna Willis
Cover design by Kevin R. Brown
Cover illustration © by Fiona King
Interior illustrations by Llewellyn art department
Revised edition editing by Kimberly Nightingale

Llewellyn is a registered trademark of Llewellyn Worldwide, Ltd.

Library of Congress Cataloging-in-Publication Data
Cunningham, Scott, 1956–1993
     Earth power.

     (Llewellyn's practical magick series)
     Bibliography: p. 171.
     ISBN 13: 978-0-87542-121-6
     ISBN 10: 0-87542-121-0
     1. Magic. 2. Charms. I. Title. II. Series.
     BF1611.C86 1983   133.4   83-81244

Llewellyn Publications
A Division of Llewellyn Worldwide, Ltd.
2143 Wooddale Drive, Dept. 978-0-87542-121-6
Woodbury, MN 55125-2989, U.S.A.
www.llewellyn.com
Printed in the United States of America

For Dave

CONTENTS

PART III: Natural Magic

ACKNOWLEDGMENTS

Many people aided in the creation of this book, as well as my own magical evolution. Among them—friends and teachers—are John and Elaine, Morgan, Ginny, Don, Donald, Morgana, Juanita, Ed and Marilee, La Dora, Judith, Raven, and many others, all who have given of their time and knowledge toward the ultimate completion of this work.

Thanks are also in order to Don Kraig, Juanita Peterson and David Harrington for supplying valuable criticism of the manuscript, and also to Mr. Harrington for proofreading.

PREFACE

From the earliest years of my life, I have been attracted to nature in all its manifestations. The sight of a field of blooming wildflowers, the texture of a granite cliff, the untameable fury of a prairie thunderstorm—these are some of my most vivid childhood impressions.

While my peers tossed around footballs or investigated the mysteries of engines and carburetors, I gazed into the night sky, attempting to comprehend its vastness. In contemplating that immensity, I felt awe and even fear. Questions regarding its blackness and the points of light within it led to other questions concerning the natural world I love.

When I discovered that even science lacked answers for many of my most probing questions, I turned my life toward explaining and solving some of these natural mysteries.

In my search for answers I came across half-forgotten religions and magical systems born in far-distant corners of the globe. Snippets of information came to light in ancient clay texts and magical treatises. When I found magic, I knew I was close. For here were practices that used the forces of nature.

I poured all my attention into investigating the myriad forms of magic. I became acquainted with magicians and Witches who furthered my learning with their arcane teachings. After many years I finally realized that the ways of magic are revealed to those who work with the forces of nature. The secrets are written in meandering streams and drifting clouds; they are whispered by the roaring ocean and cooling breeze; they echo in caves and rocks and forests.

Magic may well be the oldest extant science, yet it is also the most misunderstood practice in our world—even by some who profess to be magicians.

Magic is the art of working with the forces of nature to bring about necessary changes. That is magic, pure and simple.

The forces of nature—as they are expressed in the earth, air, fire, and water—predate our appearance on this planet. These forces could be thought of as spiritual ancestors who paved the way for our emergence from the prehistoric seas of creation.

Attuning and working with these energies in magic not only lends you the power to effect dramatic changes in your life, it also allows you to sense your own place in the larger scheme of nature. Perhaps this is the most satisfying of the fruits reaped by natural magicians.

My quest for knowledge led me to delve deeply into the magic of the earth. I have used the old ways to better my life as well as to deepen my understanding of its value and purpose. No less can be done by anyone who makes the attempt.

The tools and powers lie around us waiting to be grasped and utilized. With their help we can grow to our greatest potential.

This isn't accomplished by conquering and subduing the earth. By listening to our planet's melodies and merging with them, we become true magicians, making our magic in harmony with all nature.

Through natural magic I have found the answers to many of my questions. This book, however, is not an explanation of natural magic—that would be useless. It is a guide to the practice itself. Anyone who uses it will discover their own answers.

INTRODUCTION

This is a book of folk magic—the magic of the common people. As such, it is different from nearly every other published work on the subject.

It is not concerned with inscribing symbols on waxen pentacles, nor with raising flashing swords in triple circles, nor with invoking terrible spirits in deserted caves. This book is concerned with simpler, less complex magic.

These are the ways descended from the common folk, in the days when nearly everyone grew grain and vegetables, raised animals, spun and wove cloth and made clothing—when everything one could desire was readily at hand, could be made, or was obtainable by trade.

Men, women, and children worked from dawn to dusk in order to eat and maintain shelter. Everything in their world was handmade. So, too, was their religion and magic.

These people were of the earth. They lived, breathed, and worked with it every day. And they have left a legacy that is only now being rediscovered: natural magic.

In this book are some of the ways the magic of nature has been practiced. These are spells involving the sea, rivers, and springs; the sun and moon; storms and rain; trees and knots and mirrors.

Here is magic that anyone can perform with surprising results, for magic works!

But this is more than a spell book, for much lies behind the words on these pages. The real mysteries of magic are those of nature. In practicing these spells one touches nature, and in this work anyone can discover the secrets.

Nature, the earth, the universe, are the great initiators. It is to these that we must look for help in opening our eyes to see what has been there all the time.

Part I

BASICS

1

TOUCHING THE EARTH

The moon glows mystically in the star-scattered sky as a lone figure moves down a deserted beach.

The figure stops, bends, and grasps a gray stick washed up on the shore by the restless sea. Pushing the stick's blunt end into the wet sand, the figure sketches a symbol.

A wave crashes. The figure moves back, and just as the oncoming water sweeps over the symbol, a gust of wind rises, blowing back the tightly wrapped scarf. A woman's face appears in the soft moonlight.

She smiles, confident that the spell has worked, and sits listening to the crashing music of the sea.

Why did the woman go to the ocean that night? Why did she draw a symbol on the sand? And how did these simple acts constitute magic?

Natural magic—rather, the magic of nature—is an uncomplicated, direct branch of the magical arts, one derived from eons of experimentation by peoples scattered over the globe. It is perhaps a response to the limitless powers of nature, the power visible in the ever-changing seasons, the blossoming of a bud, the birth of young.

The ways of nature magic are almost universally intended to work with the forces and energies of nature to bring about necessary changes. Though the techniques may seem to be oversimplified, even juvenile, they are effective.

The woman described above performed an act of nature magic. She worked with the ocean, a timeless source of energy revered and worshipped for hundreds of thousands of years. To direct the energies of the sea, she used a symbol. Symbolism—the language of magic and the subconscious mind—is a sort of magical shorthand. Though the symbols and runes have powers in themselves, they also, in effect, direct energies to specific ends. In other words, they tell the magic what to do.

So this woman went to the ocean on a moonlit night to tap into oceanic energies and drew a symbol on the sand to focus powers. When the wave washed the symbol away, it released its own powers and, thusly, the magic had begun.

Though it may take several days for the fruits of the night's work to appear, they will undoubtedly do so. Time and experience will have proved this.

Natural magic is direct and to the point. Despite what you may have heard, magic is nothing supernatural, unnatural, or even alien. It is in our own backyards, our homes; in the very essence of our beings. The forces of nature empower magic, not demons and imps, "Satan," or fallen angels.

One of the greatest mysteries of magic is that there are no mysteries. Instead, the mysteries are constantly revealed around us. The study of a simple rose blossom, blade of grass, veined leaf, or whistle of wind through leafy trees will reveal as much, if not more, concerning the true nature of magic than will a hundred dusty Renaissance tomes.

It is this magic that fills these pages. While it may seem that some of the arts contained within this book fall outside of nature—mirror magic—for instance, it is simply an indication that nature is more than the good solid earth beneath our feet, or the arching rainbow dazzling an afternoon sky.

Nature is the universe itself. Not only its powers but also its manifestations. Some of these manifestations, such as mirrors, are artificially produced, but they are linked with and tap into the powers of nature by their symbolism.

In our increasingly mechanized age, many people are finding themselves isolated from the planet that sustains and supports their very lives. Forgotten is the very real dependency we have on the earth. Many people unconsciously sever their natural connections with the earth. As a result, a time of great turmoil exists today on an individual and global level.

Earth magic can help to sort out, work through, and solve many of the minor crises and problems facing us as individuals today. True, earth magic is not a simple solution to the world's problems, but it can bring order into our lives, and that's a good start.

In magical thought the human body is the "microcosm" (small representation) of the earth, which is the "macrocosm." The earth is also the microcosm of the universe. In other words, we are pictures of the essence of the planet and, thusly, of the universe. As such, when we change ourselves, we change the earth and the universe.

Magic is useful in effecting such changes in our lives, and, therefore, of the earth itself.

These changes must be positive. No evil or negative magic is contained in this book, for enough negativity already exists in the world.

The goal of all magic, occult paths, and mystical religions is the perfection of self. While this may not be accomplished in one lifetime, bettering ourselves is easily within our grasp. With this singular act, the earth becomes that much healthier.

If you put into practice any of the magic contained in this book, whether drawing a heart in the sand, gazing into a mirror for a glimpse of the future, or tying a knot to help a troubled friend, keep in mind the higher aspects of your workings. You are improving the world and helping to heal it of the terrible ravages it has suffered at our hands.

It is this which makes the practitioner of natural magic truly divine.

2

MAGIC SPELLED OUT

Magic is the use of the natural forces of nature to bring about needed changes.

To help attract, arouse, and direct these energies the magician makes use of tools. These can be costly items such as jewel-encrusted daggers and gleaming silver censers, or natural objects such as twigs and rocks. The tools necessary for this book are those of nature. Stones, trees, rivers, leaves, and plants make up the tool roster of nature magic, as well as a few store-bought items such as mirrors, candles, and cords.

The manipulation of these tools, coupled with a driving need, is often enough to work the magic; to get some of the powers of nature rolling to bring about your needed change. Magic is deceptively simple and incredibly easy, a fact that should be kept in mind while reading these pages.

Obviously, planting a stone in the ground, holding a leaf, or drawing a picture of an automobile, in and of themselves, do nothing.

It is when such actions are performed in an emotionally charged state that changes are wrought and magic is truly done.

To perform effective magic, three necessities must be present: the need, the emotion, and the knowledge.

Three Necessities

The need is simple. You wake up one morning with a splitting headache you can't get rid of. Or you may find out you need a hundred dollars by the end of the month. A friend may be looking for a new love. In all cases, a need exists.

Need should not be confused with desire. Desires are often passing; what one desires one morning may be pushed aside the next morning for something else. A desire is a whim; a need is a deeply felt, important, all-consuming state.

The emotion, too, is clear. You may need a job, for instance, but if you are not emotionally involved in the seeking of employment, worried or anxious or fretting, all the spells in the world won't bring it to you.

This is why it is sometimes fruitless to do spells for others, unless you can feel the same need that they feel emotionally.

The knowledge constitutes the body of magical lore. In other words, a spell or ritual, or the basic theories behind them, which allow you to make your own.

A spell or ritual is simply one way of doing something. There are many ways, and many possible variations on each spell. The basic principles are easy and will be discussed throughout this book.

With these three necessities, anything can be accomplished, limited only by our experience and time. The former is the key—only by performing magic will you know whether it works or not.

Magic is somewhat similar to an unknown footbridge. At first you'll step lightly on it, testing, seeing if it is safe.

After a while, you'll stride over it confidently, knowing where to step and what to avoid.

Many people approach magic with suspicion; ready to believe, but unable to do so without proof.

This is healthy. Belief is one thing, but certain knowledge is quite another. With a belief there exists the possibility that it may not be true. Certain knowledge, however, is just that—the fruits of experience that allow you to accept something completely.

Limitations—doubts and false beliefs—are crushed only through hard work and perseverance. Many people feel it is worth the effort, but this is purely a personal choice.

Magical Morality

Morality? In magic?

Yes. Not in the sense of values and ethics, whether societal or personal, for such are ever-changing—rather, morality in the spiritual sense.

Magic should be worked for positive effects, never for negative effects. The manipulation of power to cause illness, pain, death, to destroy, steal or otherwise harm another person's property, or to control other people is negative magic.

The latter includes forcing someone to fall in love with you or someone else, forcing someone to have sex with you, breaking up a marriage or romance, changing another person's mind, or forcing a person to do something they don't want to do.

Magic isn't an open field where egos and selfish urges can be gratified on a whim. There are dangers awaiting anyone who performs negative workings. Such magic might manifest, but the heavy penalties are never worth the effects.

There is a magical principle that what you put into magic is exactly what you will receive. If you perform beneficial magic, you shall receive beneficence back. The negative magician, however, shall receive only negativity, and eventually it will destroy its wielder.

In light of this principle there seems to be no reason to perform negative magic (which is often termed "black magic"). Indeed, there isn't. Those who remain unconvinced and do so, shall receive the fruits of their actions.

It is, of course, the beneficial aspect of magic that makes it and its user divine.

Negative magic has always had its adherents. There are those people who are seduced by evil—blinded by the temporary power it offers them—who can't see the light until it is too late.

Some of the magic in this book is destructive, and this may cause some confusion. Most of us connect destruction with evil. The destruction of negativity itself, however, such as bad habits, obsessions, diseases, and so on—isn't negative. Since this harms none but rather actually helps, it is safe to view it as positive magic.

Magic for the Self

Magic performed for yourself is not selfish, for it betters the world. Many people seem to think it is fine to cast a spell for a friend but would never do anything for themselves.

This is a regrettable idea, and should be exorcised as soon as possible. Only if you are healthy, happy, and financially sound can you help others, just as you must love yourself before you can expect others to love you.

Part of the confusion comes from techniques used. Magic that aids you but harms another should be avoided, for it is not in keeping with magical morality.

Usually there is a way to improve yourself or your life without harming others, and this is the magic that should be utilized.

Never feel greedy when performing magic for yourself, as long as it harms none.

Magic for Others

If you make your magical activities known, others will come to you and ask for spells to be performed. You will have to make a decision whether or not to do the magic for them, and this decision must be based upon a few factors.

There is only one hard and fast rule when it comes to working magic for others: if it feels good, do it. If not, don't.

People can be quite cagey when asking for magic to be performed. Often they'll color their explanations, or openly lie, to convince you to work.

Even good friends may fail to see the truth in some matters, or might blow one incident out of proportion. Based on such evidence, you might well tackle a problem magically that doesn't even exist, thereby wasting your time and energy.

People will also want you to accomplish something by magic that they could do themselves if they rolled up their sleeves and went to work.

With all these unsaid thoughts, hidden truths, lies, and deception, what can you do?

In magic, it is best to perform an act of divination to get some answers.

Divination

Divination is a magical process whereby the unknown becomes known. It is performed with a host of tools—mirrors, clouds, tea leaves, coffee grounds, tarot cards, dust, wind—nearly anything that can be used as an instrument of the subconscious, or psychic, mind.

Another type of divination lets the powers of the universe determine the future through moving objects or symbols.

To those of us who are not consciously, willfully psychic, divination allows us to see the future if only for a few fleeting moments. Through the use of random patterns, reflections or other focal points, psychic impulses—which are always being received by our subconscious mind—are allowed to trickle to the conscious mind, and thereby become known.

Divination also entails the use of several objects that are then manipulated, either by the magician or by forces of nature themselves, to reveal the future. These include stones, flowers, and flames. Some forms of divination use both methods.

Divination serves a very important role in magic, for it allows us to know all the circumstances surrounding a situation, especially one for which a friend wants you to work magic. Thusly, it enables us to make rational decisions whether or not to do the magic based on more complete information.

Before any magical operation, generally speaking, divination should be done to ensure that the need is there, the emotion is sufficient, and that the knowledge is certain and correct.

But divination isn't limited strictly to magical questions. It can be used as a guide to everyday problems that crop up in life.

Most of the methods are short and, with practice, should give you results.

Since there are many different methods of divination, it is best to experiment with several until you find one that works for you. Many methods are discussed in this book.

One word of caution: divination, when used to look into the future, outlines possible events. If you don't like what you see, take action to change your life before the future becomes the present.

The Power Hand

Magic speaks of the power produced by the body, which is used in some spells and rituals. This is that part of the universal energy that maintains our bodies. Some of this power is released by the emotional state achieved while performing magic and is sent along with the other energies you have raised to bring your need into manifestation.

The power hand is the hand through which these forces are released. This is the hand you write with. If you are ambidextrous, and can use either hand, choose one hand and stick with it.

This hand is used in magic to present, hold, throw, or otherwise perform in a ritualistic way a portion of a spell.

It is best to use the hand you write with where called for in specific rituals, because this is a skilled hand and it is thought that energies are naturally released through it. Thus, if you drew a symbol representing your need with your power hand, the symbol itself would be infused with a bit of your energy.

These have been the basics of magic.

It has been said that magic was the first religion, and that if you lovingly utilize the forces of nature to cause beneficial change, you also become one with them.

It is these powers that have been personified as gods and goddesses.

Attuning with them is a spiritual experience and is the basis of all true religion.

3

TECHNIQUES

The techniques required to perform natural magic are simple and easily learned. How adept you become at them rests solely on your willingness to practice. As with anything else, magic usually comes easier with practice.

This chapter is made up of short, unconnected passages dealing with some of the things you will be called upon to do in this book.

Putting all the instructions in one chapter saves constant repetition throughout the work.

Any questions raised by this chapter will be answered later in the book, when actual rituals and spells are discussed.

Symbolism

Since the subconscious mind works through symbols, it is important to cultivate the ability to interpret these symbols to decipher their meaning.

No one but you knows—really knows—what symbols mean to you. They are very personal things, dredged up from your subconscious mind, and others' interpretations can be quite wrong.

A look at some traditional symbolism, however, could be helpful in showing just how symbolism works, and how the code can be unlocked using the tool of the mind thought.

If you lit a fire, waited until its flames were quenched, and stared at its coals (see chapter 7: Fire Magic) you might see the shape of a turtle.

This is a symbol. To discover its meaning, you can look it up in this chapter, or in other books on symbolism, but that is the least trustworthy road to take.

Instead, look at the symbol itself. A turtle. What immediately comes to mind? A slow-moving creature. Perhaps aquatic. Hard-shelled, able to retreat within to escape the outside world, and fertile—many turtles lay hundreds of eggs.

That's quite a lot of turtle associations. Your next task is to look at these associations in connection with a question you asked. If you asked why you couldn't seem to hold onto a love, perhaps your psychic mind is saying that you've been acting like a turtle—dull, slow-moving, always retreating from the world.

Look only at those qualities of the symbol that relate to your question. Soon, you will have an answer.

If you didn't ask a question, determine possible future events the same way, by taking those associations from the symbol and applying them to your life. You will come up with an answer.

While this process is sometimes difficult, and requires time and work, it is one of the basic components of any divinatory act—once you have the symbols or pictures, they must be interpreted.

This section will hopefully serve as a guideline. Remember that these are suggested meanings for some commonly seen symbols. If you are in violent disagreement with any of them, stick to your own intuition—that's best of all.

ACORN: men, youth, strength

AIRPLANE: travel, new projects

ANCHOR: voyage, rest

ARROW: news

BASKET: gift

BABY: new interests

BEES, HONEY COMB, HIVE: industry, frugality, hard work

BELL: celebrations, marriage (Bells ring in the new but also ring out the old. The bell may be tolling hard times as well.)

BIRD: psychic powers, flight, movement, motion, good luck

BOAT: discoveries

BOOK: wisdom

BROOM: cleanliness, femininity, domesticity, purification, healing, warfare with negativity

BUTTERFLY: frivolous things, nonessentials

CAGE, PRISON BARS: restriction, isolation, solitude

CAT: wisdom, intellectualism, aloofness

CAULDRON: transformation, great change, women, new beginnings, endings

CLOCK: death, time in any manifestation, change

CLOUDS: headaches, mental problems, the mind, thoughts

COFFIN: Surprise! It's not death. Instead, a long and boring but not serious illness.

COW: money, prosperity

CRADLE: strangers

CRESCENT: freshness, newness, mother, women

CORNUCOPIA: fertility, protection, prosperity, animals, containment

CROSS: equal-armed—the forces of nature, the elements, great energies at work; Christian—religion, consolation, suffering

CROWN: success

DISTAFF: creativity, change, sexuality, transformation

DOG: love, friend, fidelity

DUCK: wealth, plenty

EGG: increase, fertility, luck

EYE: introspection, inspection, evaluation

FISH: sexuality, riches, lucky speculation

FLAME, FIRE: purification, change, the will, domination, driving forces

GLOVE: luck, protection

GUN, PISTOL, RIFLE: discord, disaster, slander

HAT: rival, honors

HEART: love, pleasure

HORNS: fertility, godliness, spirituality, forces of nature

HORSE: strength, travel, grace

HORSESHOE: luck, protection, travel

HOUR GLASS: caution

HOUSE: success

HUMMINGBIRD: communication, visitors

KEY: mysteries, enlightenment, security, prosperity, fertility

KNOT: manifestation, hindrance, marriage, binding, restriction

LADDER: turmoil, sun, ascent, descent, evolution, initiation

LION: influence, royalty, power, strength, ferocity

LOCK: obstacles, protection, safety, security

MIRROR: reversal, moon, women, love, reflection, beauty, knowledge, transference, communication

MOUNTAIN: journeys, hindrances

MOUSE: poverty, theft

MUSHROOM: shelter, food

NAIL: pain, anguish

OWL: wisdom

PARROT: brashness, color, scandal

PEACOCK: luxury, splendor, vanity

PINEAPPLE: hospitality, easy life

PINE CONES: food, sustenance, winter

PURSE: gain, money

RING: marriage, containment, eternity

ROSE: love, lost love, richness of life, the past

SALT: purity, purification, money, stability, foundation, cleansing, healing

SCALES: balance, justice

SCISSORS: quarrels, separations

SHELL: creativity, good luck, money, prosperity, emotional stability

SHIP: increase, travel, news

SKULL AND CROSSBONES: death, resurrection, comfort, consolation

SNAKE: wisdom, eternity, masculinity, a man, secrecy, knowledge

SPIDER: very good fortune, cunning, secrecy, hidden things, money

SPOON: luck

STAR: excellent luck, divine protection, fortune, wealth, high honors, respectability, success

SWAN: good luck, a lover

SWORD: life, death, conflicts, arguments, negativity

TREE: good luck, forces of nature, age, stability, power

TRIANGLE: one point up—good luck; one point down—bad luck

TURTLE: sluggishness, fertility, retreat, stagnation

WELL: spirituality, inspiration, Mother Nature, love

WHEEL: seasons, reincarnation, completion, endings, forever

Remember that these are suggestions only. I can't tell you exactly what an American flag would mean to you, any more than you could know the personal meaning of a goat to me. The secret of symbols is revealed to those who work with them by your own mind.

Imagination and Visualization

This is exactly what it sounds like. Imagination is the origin of all things that humans have produced. It is this vital tool that will be at work in magic more than any other.

Imagination is a must in divination (see chapter 2: Magic Spelled Out) in unlocking symbolism. Imagination is also necessary in visualizing exactly what you need while performing a work of magic.

Imagination is not uncontrolled mental rambling. Like the product of a skilled artist who with brush and paints produces a finished, complete picture, imagination can be used like those paints and brushes to produce a perfect image of your need.

Imagination is the ability to use your mind creatively. The word "creative" is linked with "creation." In a very real sense you "create" what you imagine, or visualize, as it is also known. This is one of the basics of magic—the visualization—and this is done through imagination.

Surely, at this moment, you could visualize a warm Hawaiian beach, even if you've never been to the islands. You could also visualize a daisy, or a telephone.

In magic, imagination is used to visualize the need.

If, for some reason, visualization of the need isn't possible, visualize a symbol that matches it. A dove for peace, perhaps, or a rose for love.

Scrying

One of the most common forms of divination, scrying is simply looking at, into, or onto a vessel, surface, or material. There is a wide variety of scrying methods included in this book, utilizing everything from fire to water.

The secret of scrying is relaxation. If you sit tensely, your eyes rushing around desperately trying to find symbols, you will fail.

Relax and look. They will come to you.

This may sound too simple, but it is true. Some methods work better than others, and so practical experimentation is necessary to find the one that works best for you.

Scrying works because of various factors. The random patterns present in heaps of earth, or the ripples of a stream, or the glowing coals of a dying fire, allow the conscious mind to relax its hold, giving up total control and allowing the subconscious mind to whisper in your ear, pointing out symbols with which you can unlock the answer to your questions, or glimpse your future.

It can be quite effective with practice.

Concentration

Concentration is an extremely potent form of magic. Concentration—retaining a thought or image or picture in the mind without interruption of other data or ideas—is central to many spells and rituals.

The logic is clear that what is held in the mind and concentrated upon is being given power. If you concentrate on your need, for instance, while tying a leaf to a tree, you add your power (raised by the mind) to the spell.

Positive thinking is one example of the power that the mind can have upon the world. We know that the telephone, airplane, electric lamp, and everything humans have created began as thoughts. The thought was held (concentration) until it could be put into manifestation (creation).

In a similar way, we hold a thought (the need), and while doing this, use the emotion and the knowledge to bring our need into manifestation (creation).

If we do not concentrate on our need, the emotion falters, the knowledge is useless and powerless, and we'd be better off never having started the spell in the first place.

Concentration is a vital part of any spell. Though some people have difficulty with concentration due to our fast-moving world, a simple exercise, if persisted in, will do wonders.

At night, isolated from other people, light, and noises, light a plain white candle and lie or sit comfortably before it.

Relax your body and gaze at the candle's flame, shutting out any other thoughts.

If you can manage to think of nothing but the candle shining in the dark for more than a few minutes, you are well on your way.

Feeling the Power

What power? Not the energy piped through your home, but the powers of magic—the forces of the elements and winds, the energy that keeps our planet spinning within our spinning galaxy within a spinning universe. This is the real energy of magic.

One of the best ways to gain a familiarity with this power is through memory. We have the power at all times; it is what keeps our body running and working properly. We take it in through the food we eat and release it in physical exertion, mental workings, and simple bodily functions like breathing and blinking our eyes.

Since this power is with us at all times, it sometimes makes its presence known.

Most people have experienced a thunderstorm. Jagged lightning glances across the sky, rain and wind slam down, and the sky shakes with tremendous thunder. Such a storm will often cause unexpected reactions.

A chill might shake you, both in anxiety and also in exhilaration of such a spectacular example of nature's unlimited power.

If you can recall an especially powerful storm that sent a chill down your spine, attempt to recapture that feeling. Recall the time; remember your reactions to the storm.

You may begin to feel charged with energy. Your pulse and breathing may increase in rate, the muscles of your body may tense, and you may begin to perspire.

These physical changes are manifestations of the increased amount of energy surging through your body.

This is the same energy used in magic. As mentioned previously, much of the energy is generated by the emotion. Emotional reactions to situations can have amazing results (the weak woman who pushed a car off her child's leg, for example) that seem to defy normal laws.

This isn't the case. These power surges are manifestations of other laws of nature not yet discovered by science.

Since emotion is an excellent way in which to feel the power, a strong emotional reaction—such as that to a storm—is often beneficial to help the power begin flowing.

Obviously it would be ridiculous to stand and reexperience a thunderstorm before every spell. Simply use the thunderstorm exercise in order to feel the energy—the energy that manifests itself in tense muscles, increased respiration and heart rates, and perhaps perspiration.

Once you have felt it and can do so at will, you can generate power and send it off during your spells to work your need.

Any spell performed in such a state will be much more effective than one that was walked through.

Again, use the emotion of the need of the particular spell to attain this state. If you desperately need five hundred dollars for an unexpected, neglected, or forgotten bill, pour all of your concern into the spell. But back it up with your unshakeable knowledge that you can and will draw it to you.

All right, so it isn't easy at first. As my piano teacher used to tell me, "Practice!"

4

THE ELEMENTS OF MAGIC

The elements within magical symbolism are the basic components of all that exists. These four elements—earth, air, fire, and water—are at the same time visible and invisible, physical and spiritual.

From these elements all things have been fashioned, according to magical thought. Our current scientific knowledge, which states that there are many more such "building blocks," isn't unharmonious with this statement, but is merely a more refined version of the four element concept.

It is unwise to view the four elements in purely physical terms. Earth, for example, refers not only to the planet on which we exist, but also to the phenomenon of earthiness, of foundation, and stability. Similarly, fire is much more than flame.

While there are many attributes to these elements that are out of place in this chapter, a few words on each of them and why they are important in magical workings is necessary.

Since this is the magic of nature, using natural powers, tools, and symbols, it is important to understand these powers. One of the ways this can be achieved is through the study of the elements.

The elemental system was devised and refined in the Renaissance, but its roots stretch farther back into history. It can be viewed as nothing more than a convenient system of organization for the various types of magic. Then again, it may be viewed as a very real system of powers that can be called upon to aid spells and rituals. How you view the elements is up to you.

The following discussions deal with the symbolism of and types of magic related to the elements. All of the magic contained within this book falls under the rulership of one (or more) of the elements. This is true, too, of all that exists.

An understanding of the elements will aid your magical work immensely.

Though the elements are described as "masculine" or "feminine," this should not be viewed in a sexist way. This, like all magical systems, is symbolic—it describes the basic attributes of the elements in terms easily understandable. It doesn't mean that it is more masculine to perform fire magic, or more appropriate for women to use water magic. It's simply a system of symbols.

Earth

This is the element we are closest to home with, since it is our home. Earth doesn't necessarily represent the physical earth, but that part of it which is stable, solid, and dependable.

Earth is the foundation of the elements, the base. It is in this realm that most of us live a good part of our lives. When we walk, sit, stand, crawl, eat, sleep, work our jobs, tend our plants, balance our checkbooks or taste salt we are working within the element of earth.

Earth is the realm of abundance, prosperity, and wealth. While it is the most physical of the elements this is not negative, for it is upon earth that the other three rest. Without earth, life as we know it could not exist.

In magical workings, earth "rules" all spells and rituals involving business, money, employment, prosperity in all its forms, stability, fertility, and so on.

A ritual of this element could be as simple as burying an object representative of your need in a plot of virgin ground, walking over miles of countryside visualizing your need, or drawing images in dirt.

Earth is a feminine element. It is nurturing, moist, and fruitful, and it is these qualities that make it feminine. Such attributes have impelled countless civilizations to envision the earth as a great Mother Goddess, the all-fertile Creatress of nature.

Earth rules the northern point of the compass, because that is the place of greatest darkness and of winter. Its color is the green of the fields and plants.

It governs stone, image, tree, and knot magic.

Air

Air is the element of the intellect; it is the realm of thought, which is the first step toward creation.

Magically speaking, air is the clear, uncluttered, pure visualization that is a powerful tool for change. It is also movement, the impetus that sends the visualization out toward manifestation.

It rules spells and rituals involving travel, instruction, freedom, obtaining knowledge, discovering lost items, uncovering lies, and so on.

It can also be used to develop the psychic faculties.

Spells involving air usually include the act of placing an object in the air or dropping something off the side of a mountain or other high place so that the object actually connects physically with the element.

Air is a masculine element, being dry, expansive, and active. It is the element that excels in places of learning, and which is at work while we theorize, think, and ponder.

Air rules the east because this is the direction of the greatest light, and the light of wisdom and consciousness. Its color is yellow, the yellow of the sun and of the sky at dawn, and its season is spring.

Air governs the magic of the four winds, most divinations, concentration and visualization magic.

Fire

Fire is the element of change, will, and passion. In a sense it contains within it all forms of magic, since magic is a process of change.

Fire magic can be frightening. The results manifest quickly and spectacularly. It is not an element for the faint-hearted. It is most primal, however, and for this reason is much used.

This is the realm of sexuality and passion. It is not only the "sacred fire" of sex, it is also the spark of divinity that shines within us and in all living things. It is at once the most physical and spiritual of the elements.

Its magical rituals usually involve energy, authority, sex, healing, destruction (of negative habits, disease), purification, evolution, and so on.

A ritual of fire usually involves the fuming, burning, or smouldering of an image, herb, or other flammable object, or the use of candles or small blazes.

Its magic is usually practiced near the hearth, or beside fires lit in wilderness clearings, or beside the flame of a single candle.

Fire is masculine. It rules the south, the place of greatest heat, the color red, and the season of summer.

All candle magic comes under fire's powers.

Water

Water is the element of purification, the subconscious mind, love, and the emotions.

Just as water is fluid, constantly changing, flowing from one level to another, so too are our emotions in a constant state of flux.

Water is the element of absorption and germination. The subconscious is symbolized by this element because it is rolling, always moving, like the sea that rests neither night or day.

Water magic involves pleasure, friendship, marriage, fertility, happiness, healing, sleep, dreaming, psychic acts, purification, and so on.

A ritual of water usually ends with an object being tossed or placed in or on a body of water.

This is a feminine element, and its color is the blue of deep, deep water. It rules the west and autumn months of the year, when rain showers wash the earth.

The magic of water is wrought with mirrors, the sea, fog and rain.

These, then, are the four elements. A thorough study of them can occupy a lifetime, but these are the basics.

Though it isn't necessary to call upon these elements or to work with them directly, it is beneficial to be aware of them and to remember them while working magic.

For actual workings with the elements, see the next four chapters.

Part II

ELEMENTAL
MAGIC

5

EARTH MAGIC

Earth is our only home. It is that from which mythologically we sprang, and in its moist soil we bury our deceased. From its surface we pull verdant vegetables and healing plants. Animals graze atop it, and within it lie riches of gold and silver, precious stones and oil. Until recently, no living thing—save birds—left its surface for more than a few moments.

The ancient goddesses of the earth have survived to this day in the guise of Mother Nature, a deity being reclaimed by nature-conscious souls in the dawning of the twenty-first century. The earth was once worshipped for its own sake, and today it is newly revered as our home and our sustenance; without it we would perish.

Ecological movements have sprung up to fill the need of protecting our planet. Spaceship Earth, as it came to be called once we had succeeded in leaving its atmosphere and gazed at its bluish mass from space, is Gaia: our Mother, our home, our all. It always has been.

As such, it has entered into religious and magical thought and practice for thousands of years. Some of the spells and techniques presented in this chapter are as ageless as the thrust of a mountain. In these earthy spells lie the roots of all magic, for if all forms of magic are not of this element, they are certainly performed upon the earth.

Think of a freshly dug handful of earth. Smell the richness of the fertile soil. See the striking color, from whitest clay to volcanic red to blackest black. This is the fertilizing nature, the storehouse of vitamins and minerals essential to life. This is also an excellent arena in which (or with which) to practice magic.

Here is some of that magic.

TO HEAL

Healing with the earth works through the process of transference. The wound or disease is transferred magically to another substance, usually an organic one, which is then buried. As it rots, it releases the wound or disease.

To remove a disease or heal a wound, rub the afflicted part with an apple or potato. Then, as quickly as possible, dig a hole in the ground, put it in, and cover it over with earth. It is done.

One note here might be wise. Healing magic should always be used in addition to conventional medicine and never as a replacement. Doctors are the only people qualified to help your body heal itself.

By all means perform healing magic for yourself or friends, but not in place of qualified medical attention. The medicine of today was the magic of yesterday.

THE EARTH BED

If you are sick, find a spot where the earth is bare, uncovered by concrete, plants, and leaves—pure fresh soil.

Sit or lie down on the earth. Mentally see your wound or disease sinking into the earth. Feel the pain and anguish, the physical and emotional effects of the problem running down into the ground beneath you.

Sense the rhythm of the earth—feel the steady beat of nature pounding away. It should pulsate in tune with your heart, pounding until you feel your whole body undulating with energy.

Then feel it coming—cool, deep, soft energy rising from the ground up into you.

Rise, dust yourself off, and check to see if you feel different.

If you are bedridden or otherwise cannot do this, have a dish or pot of fresh soil in your sickroom. Earth gives off healing vibrations and its presence will aid your recovery.

A simple method would be to place a potted plant in your sickroom. Not only will the plant lend its own healing energies (ivy is great and will cause no strange looks) but the soil in which it is placed will aid you as well.

TO LOSE YOUR TROUBLES

Take a handful of earth and gaze into it; pour into it all your problems. Outline, in minute detail, all of those problems plaguing you.

When you are finished, throw the dirt behind you and walk away from it, not turning back.

AN EARTH CHARM

Tie up in a small green square of cloth some fresh, rich soil.

Firmly tie this so no earth can escape.

Carry this with you if you have troubles with stability, security, and self-control. If you are apt to let your emotions rule your life or if you are constantly angry or nervous, this amulet of earth will help.

EARTH SCRYING

Fill a small flat vessel at least seven inches in diameter with earth. Sit relaxed and gaze not only at, but into the soil. You will eventually begin to notice symbols staring up from the earth.

AN EARTH PROTECTION BOTTLE

Into a long, small bottle pour fresh, clean soil. Fill it to the top and cap it. Place this bottle near the entrance, preferably in a window, to guard against evil entering into your home.

In past ages earth was thought to confound evil spirits and demons, who had to count every grain of earth in the bottle before entering the dwelling.

Today, evil spirits are seen as negativity that floats around the earth in large quantities. This negativity can enter your home. This earth protection bottle can, therefore, be useful in blocking negativity from entering your house.

TO PROTECT CHILDREN

To protect them while you are away, throw a handful of earth or sand after them as they leave, without their knowledge. This will ensure their safety.

A LONG-TERM EARTH SPELL

This spell is ideal if you are a good gardener, and if you have a need that you don't mind waiting several months before it manifests.

Take a seed from a plant that is symbolically related to your need (see appendix III). Over a pot of soil or a special plot of land, hold the seed in your power hand and visualize your need strongly.

Speak to the seed. Tell it why you need its help to make your need come to fruition.

Then plant the seed, giving it loving encouragement and water.

Tend to the seedling when it appears and be sure that the plant doesn't die due to your own neglect or carelessness. If this happens, your need won't manifest. At least not until you do another spell.

If the plant grows up healthy and happy, expect your need to arrive. Once it has, take very good care of your magical plant, for it not only represents your need, but it also is now a growing, living thing, which you brought to life in order to fulfill your need.

You are responsible for the plant. Take care of it and it will sing to you alone all the secrets of earth magic.

A VARIATION

In a plot of prepared land, sow the seeds of an appropriate plant in the form of a symbol or rune (see appendix II) representative of your need.

Tend to the garden. When the seedlings first pop up, draw a circle around the symbol in the earth with the forefinger of your power hand. Stand in quiet contemplation of the growing, living symbol of your need. As it has sprung into existence, so too shall your need.

6

AIR MAGIC

Without air, our planet would be a lifeless globe. No life as we know it could exist without the combination of gasses with which our planet is fortunately supplied.

Though air is invisible it is an essential part of life. It is not only necessary for life to continue, it also affects our lives in often dramatic ways. Since it is invisible and yet so powerful it has been used in spells and magic for eons, and it also has found its way through the winds into the folklore and mythology of peoples around the world.

The spells and techniques offered here utilize the power of elemental air, best visualized as a gushing torrent of wind. Many of the spells themselves require a wind or at least a breeze, and spells for wind control are also included.

One point of caution: air magic is as unpredictable as the winds themselves.

The Winds

For centuries peoples have thought of the wind as being of four basic types, corresponding to the four directions or quarters of the earth. These are the north, east, south, and west winds. Each is possessed of its own magical virtues, and certain spells are best cast during certain winds.

This may seem to be rather unnecessarily complicated, but it needn't be. Looking to the winds when performing magic is no more difficult than checking the phase of the moon, although the "phase" of the wind doesn't last as long.

At best, if you can rig up a weathervane or windsock to determine the winds, you can adjust your magical workings slightly by waiting for the right wind.

Naturally, if the wind has been blowing steadily from the north all morning, it won't do to wait for a westerly one. The system is here to guide and aid, not to control our actions. Check the winds or not as you wish.

In looking over the following discussions of each of the winds, bear in mind that this is not an absolute system; different parts of the world have different attributes for the winds. The attributes described below are those favored in North America and Europe. Changes may be necessary for your own area, due to climate, location, and weather patterns.

The four winds are at least superficially related to the elements, and this can be kept in mind, but each has its own powers peculiar to the winds themselves.

One important point: in speaking of, say, the north wind, it is the wind that blows from that direction rather than to the direction that is in question.

North Wind

The north wind is the wind of death—but not necessarily that of physical death. This is the realm of the one eternal universal law—change. "Death" here refers to the elimination of negativity.

The north wind is cold (magically speaking), blowing in as it does from the direction of winter when snows lie deep across the lands. It is "dry," or barren, thus paving the way for spells of destruction.

How to use it? If you are depressed, anxious, envious, jealous, angry, and the wind is blowing from the north, face full into it and it will free you of these things.

If you wish to break a bad habit, perform any spell of this, nature while the north wind is blowing for added power.

The north wind, while chilly with night and death and deep snows, is also the wind of the element earth, and thus shares in some of its qualities. But the wind, being dry, is not favorable for fertility and prosperity magic, although magic involving healing can be greatly aided by the north wind.

Its color is the black of midnight.

East Wind

The wind blowing from the east is that of freshness, renewed life, strength, power, and intellect. It is a warm, bracing wind that blows from the point at which the sun, moon, and stars make their shining appearances.

Thusly, it is the wind involved with beginnings, the new phenomena that rise from the work of the north wind. The heat is that of the sun, and the spark of creation.

Spells best utilized when the wind is sweeping from the east are those concerning dramatic improvements and changes for the better, especially in behavior. Also, east wind spells are those involving the mind and all spells involving the element of air, to which it is magically related.

Love spells are best not performed with an easterly wind, unless you want a very intellectual love. But perhaps there's nothing wrong with that!

Since the east is the direction of sunrise and light, the color is white.

South Wind

The further south you travel, the hotter it gets—on this side of the equator, at least. For this reason, the southern wind is a hot and fiery one.

Symbolically it rules noon, when the sun (or moon) is highest in the sky, the time of the greatest light and heat. Because the south wind is related to the element of fire, its magic covers the same ground. The south wind, however, can be used for any type of magic when it's blowing. It's a good time to cast spells.

Since this wind is strong and hot, spells performed with it are assured an extra jolt of power. It is always exciting and interesting working with the south wind!

Be warned, however, that fire—even the diluted fire of the southern wind—can be dangerous. As we know, fire can burn.

The color of the south wind? Yellow—the yellow of the sun at noon.

West Wind

The west wind blows cool and moist; it may carry a hint of rain or mist as it washes over the land. It is a fertile, loving force that is gentle and persuasive.

It symbolically rules twilight, when all is at a standstill; day and night merge into a magical landscape of muted colors and breezes. Sunset, like sunrise, is an excellent time to perform magic—more so if the correct wind is blowing.

Water magic—love, healing, fertility and so on—is excellent for the west wind, as it adds its own forces and energies from that quarter. Especially excellent for spells involving cleansing or purely religious rituals, the west wind is welcome relief after the dry, hot breeze from the south.

The west wind is the blue of the sky just before all light fades from the sky.

Charting the Winds

As mentioned previously, the best way to determine the winds is by a weathervane or windsock. The latter can be made cheaply in seconds and is as accurate as anything.

Take a strip of heavy but flexible cloth at least one-and-a-half feet in length (or, if you prefer, a long, clean sock) and find a good place on your property to hang it up. It should be free of surrounding buildings or trees that could block the winds. Preferably, it will be on your property and will be visible from the house.

If you lack such a spot, a rooftop antenna will do. Tie the cloth securely to the antenna (or a pole high enough to catch the wind) and insure that the wind won't blow it free or slide it down along the pole.

Now determine the directions and wait for the wind. When it blows, the cloth will stream in the opposite direction. Thus, when the cloth is streaming south, the north wind is at work.

If the windsock is visible from within your house, it will simply be a matter of looking at it, determining the wind from its condition, and proceeding from there.

INVOKING THE FOUR WINDS

Many spells and rituals can be prefaced with an invocation to the winds. This is particularly true if you are often working with the winds.

The idea of invoking or calling the winds is an ancient one, dating back to at least classical Greece and certainly earlier. It is not only a summons of their power (all four winds to help your spell) but is also a general announcement to them of your intentions. This is made, in effect, to the entire world.

Summoning the powers of the winds and asking for their help is a great way to begin any spell. The technique?

Once you have assembled everything you need for the spell in the place you are performing it (preferably outside), turn to the north and say something like the following:

Winds of the north!
Rushing and mighty!
Aid me in my magical work!

Turn to the east and say:

Winds of the east!
Dazzling and bright!
Aid me in my magical work!

Face south, and say:

Winds of the south!
Fiery and radiant!
Aid me in my magical work!

Then move to the west and say:

Winds of the west!
Gentle and buoyant!
Aid me in my magical work!

Now proceed with the spell, secure that the ancient powers of the four winds are aiding your magic.

Working with One Wind

If you are performing a spell suited to one wind, just before you begin, turn to the appropriate direction and say the words associated with it above. Stand for a moment. Feel the wind (if only in your imagination) blowing from that direction, roused by your magical call, gathering in speed as it rushes toward you with awesome force. (This is also a good thing to do while invoking all four winds.)

Then perform the spell.

Air Spells

These are some of the workings associated with the element of air. For your convenience, I have listed the appropriate wind related to each, although it is never necessary to wait until the wind is actually blowing to perform these spells.

TIE UP YOUR TROUBLES (NORTH WIND)

On a sturdy, preferably dead bush or shrub still planted in the ground, in a place where the winds blow clear and free, tie or push onto the tip of a branch or twig one leaf for every one of the ills that is bothering you. If you tie the leaf, do so loosely and use a natural fiber cord.

This is all you have to do, for the north wind will rise and, perhaps slowly, untie and free the leaves, thereby releasing energy and going to work to alleviate the ills besetting you.

This spell works over a period of days or even weeks, not minutes, so leave the shrub after performing the spell. If you wait and watch, the wind might never rise. (Of course, it gives you a head start to perform this work during a stiff north breeze!)

A LOVING BELL (WEST WIND)

Hang up a bell with a pleasant ring in a window that remains open for a good part of each day, and through which the wind blows (preferably the west wind).

As you do so, speak these words:

Little bell of love, I hang you to whisper my need for
love on the breezes and winds.

Little bell of love, speak of my need for love to your
brothers and sisters.
Little bell of love, I ask you to speak softly and draw
to me someone who listens.

Every time the bell rings, it is "whispering" of your need for
love. (The "brothers and sisters" are other bells who will add
their own power to the spell.)

TO VANQUISH FEAR (SOUTH WIND)

Light a yellow candle indoors and sit in quiet contemplation
for a second. See the candle's flames drawing in your fear and
anxieties; see it and the candle becoming infused with them.

Take the candle outside and let the wind quench its flame.
It is done.

(Check to make sure there is a breeze or wind outside before trying this one.)

TO COMMUNICATE WITH AN ABSENT FRIEND (EAST WIND)

In the open air, face the direction where the person is present.
If this is unknown, repeat the steps below to each direction,
starting in the north.

Extend your arms and hands and, in a clear but soft voice,
call the person's name.

Visualize his or her features. Call the name again, with more
force, and then a third time, quite loudly.

Next, state your message as if speaking to them in person.
Keep this short and precise. When you have finished, listen for
a reply.

Don't imagine one, but listen.

This works best with practice, or with friends with whom you are intimately close.

TO MAKE A DECISION (EAST WIND)

If you are faced with many choices, write each down on small slips of paper. Fold each twice and place them on a table that is standing free (i.e., it is not pushed up against a wall), in a place where a gentle wind is blowing.

The wind should make the papers move around on the table top, and then fall to the ground. The last paper remaining on the table (or the last to fall, if you don't catch it soon enough) is your choice, should you decide to follow it.

Determining a Wind

As you have seen, air magic can be done one of two ways: actually using the element of air through one of the above spells, invoking the correct wind or not, or by simply invoking the powers of all of the winds or one in particular and performing another type of spell.

For spells in which you wish to invoke a wind but aren't sure which is appropriate, the following spell can be used.

In a fireproof item or area, build a small fire of any type of wood. Or, use some charcoal and light it.

Next, when the fire is blazing brightly or the coals are glowing, throw green branches of trees and shrubs on the fire or coals to create smoke. The smoke should rise steadily from the fire. The fire isn't important now; only the smoke is.

Watch to see the direction the smoke travels in.

It may immediately move toward a direction, or rise straight up. If the latter occurs, keep watching and it should turn. The direction in which the smoke travels is the appropriate wind for the spell you are considering.

Granted, this is a bit of trouble, but it works.

Be sure that the fire is safely extinguished, with sand or water, before leaving the area.

To Raise the Winds

THE WEATHER STRIP

Used to raise winds at sea (to fill the sails) or on land. In an old rawhide thong of about an arm's length, tie a knot three inches from the end, a second knot six inches from the first, and a third nine inches from the second knot.

To activate the spell, untie the knots:

For a gentle breeze, untie the first knot, concentrating on waves or leaves or grass blowing.

For a stronger wind, untie the second knot, concentrating on a steady wind filling a ship's sails.

For a gale (careful!) untie the last knot, thinking of a heavy gale and lots of wind action.

It is done.

TO RAISE THE WIND

First, look to the direction suitable to the time of year:

In the winter, try the north wind.

In the spring, try the east wind.

In the summer, try the south wind.

In the autumn, try the west wind.

Turn to the appropriate direction and give a long, piercing whistle with the pitch dropping off at the end. Do this thrice.

The best time to call the wind is at sunrise.

TO RAISE WINDS

Take several handfuls of sand and throw them up into the air. By the third or fourth handful, the wind should have picked up and blown the sand from your hand. Use fine, clean sand for this spell.

TO STOP THE WIND

Gather four feathers, preferably one each of these colors: white, blue, yellow, and black to represent the four winds. Take these four feathers and tie them together tightly with a thick cord. Place the feathers in the bottom of a bowl and cover them over completely with salt so that they aren't visible.

This will bind the winds and they should soon abate.

TO STOP A CYCLONE

Run into a field and stick a knife into the ground, with the sharp edge of the blade facing the coming storm. The knife is said to "split the wind," so that your area will be spared.

TO RAISE THE WIND ON A SEASHORE

Take a long piece of seaweed, whirl it over your head in a circle, and whistle.

7

FIRE MAGIC

Fire has always sparked religious awe. Its ever-shifting form, varieties of colors, heat, and light, plus the actual physical changes it produces are the stuff magic is made of.

Before the knowledge of fire making, it must have been a dark world, indeed. With the use of friction and flints, humans captured this divine essence and it changed the world forever.

While so-called fire worship is generally nothing more than a polite euphemism for the mystical reverence of sex, there have been several religions that worshipped fire as a symbol of divinity.

Who hasn't heard of the eternal flames that the vestal virgins of rome tended on their altars? Even today, Jewish synagogues keep an eternal flame, and some tombs, like John F. Kennedy's, are similarly equipped.

Though the religious significance of fire has been forgotten by most of us today, it is still in evidence upon the altars of many of the world's leading religions. What Catholic altar would be complete without flaming candles? A candle's shining flame or a roaring bonfire on a lonely mountain peak are both objects of power that can be utilized in magic.

The fact that fire is a powerful element caused the ancients to worship it. The placement of burning candles on the altar during mass isn't accidental—those candles release their own energies into the proceedings, as does the smoking frankincense in the brightly shining censers and the prayers of the devout.

Candle magic is once again becoming enormously popular, perhaps because it is simple and effective. Though this may be the only form of fire magic readily available, it is far from the only one known today. It is these other forms that shall be investigated here. (see chapter 13: Candle Magic).

Fire magic can be performed wherever a fire can be safely lit. An indoor or outdoor fireplace, a barbecue, a cleared section of ground, or a specially dug pit lined with bricks or rocks—anything will work, as long as the fire can be safely lit in an area in which you have privacy to perform your magic.

For some spells you will need no more than a few pieces of kindling. For others, whole blazes or series of fires will be required. Any sort of fuel is fine, as long as it is clean, dry, and not too sappy.

(If you wish to add power to your fire magic, check chapter 10: Tree Magic for specific types of wood and their powers. Remember, if you harvest any wood yourself, be sure to talk to the tree, thank it for its wood, and leave an offering on the ground.)

Owing to its fiery nature, this sort of magic is best performed in the desert, but anywhere will suffice.

A PURIFICATION

If you wish to be free from a habit, thought, idea, past associations, guilt, or blockage; take the symbols of that problem—whatever it may be—and throw them onto a raging fire. The fire will consume the symbols and so shall it consume the power they had over you.

For the symbols think a moment—if you overeat, take a portion of your favorite food and throw it onto the fire. For smoking or drinking, do the same. For problems that utilize no concrete objects, draw a symbol or image and burn.

A FIRE PROTECTION SPELL

In a clear spot at least twenty feet in diameter, gather together plenty of wood, matches, and a quantity of water. Taking up one of the sticks of wood, draw a rough circle about eleven feet in diameter. Determine the directions (use a compass, the sun, moon, or stars) and lay a small fire at each point just inside the circle: north, east, south, and west.

Lay the fires, but do not light them. Next to each, place enough fuel to keep them burning at least a half hour.

Walking to the south first, light the fire, shouting these words as you do:

**Nothing from the south
can harm me!**

Move to the west.
Light the fire and say:

Nothing from the west can harm me!

At the north, light the fire while saying:

**Nothing from the north
can harm me!**

Finally, in the east, light the fire and say:

Nothing from the east can harm me!

Snatch up a burning stick from the southern fire and thrust it at the sky above you (be careful of burning ashes and sparks) and say:

Nothing from above can harm me!

Next, throw the flaming wood down onto the earth, saying:

Nothing from below can harm me!

Replace the stick in the southern fire and sit in the center of the circle, watching the fires burn. As necessary, add more fuel.

Know that the fires are literally burning away all that comes to harm you, on every level.

Firmly implant in your mind the sight of the fires burning around you, the feel of their heat (which can become intense), their light, and their protective qualities.

When the fires begin to die and you feel the power ebbing, bury the fires with earth or sand, douse with water, and obliterate the circle you've drawn on the ground.

Leave the area, but retain the fiery circle of protection within your memory, so that it can be recalled at any time you feel the need for protection: physical, spiritual, or mental.

If you are prevented from performing this ritual outdoors, substitute four large red candles for the fires. Proceed with the spell above, lighting the candles rather than the fires, until all four are lit and you have said the words.

Then, instead of taking a burning stick from the southern fire, pick up the candle in that quarter itself and hold it carefully over your head. Say the words, then place it on the ground, saying those words. When the ritual is done, pinch out the candles, beginning with the west (never blow them out).

A FIRE DIVINATION

Set a fire and watch how quickly the wood begins to burn. If it catches the flame quickly, it is a good sign, and you should proceed with the divination.

If it is hesitant, or if you need to use several matches to get even the smallest twig to light, abandon the project until another time.

Some say that if the fire lights quickly, it is a sign that visitors are on their way. Others say that if the fire is difficult to light, rain is expected.

Once the fire is actually blazing, watch its flames carefully.

If the fire burns to one side of the fireplace, pit, or area, love may be in the air.

Much crackling indicates misfortune ahead; perform protective spells.

A distinct hollow in the midst of the flames foretells an ending of a problem bothering you.

If the fire suddenly roars up the chimney or up into the air for no apparent reason, an argument may soon occur. Watch your words carefully.

Sparks on the back of the chimney or, if outside, flying aggressively up into the air mean that important news is on the way.

If a loved one is far from home, poke at the fire with a poker or stick. If shafts of flame shoot up, you can be assured that he or she is well, safe, and happy.

Finally, if three bolts of flame rise up and burn separately, expect a momentous event to occur in your life soon.

ANOTHER FIRE DIVINATION

Once the fire has died to a glowing reddish-white mass of coals, stare into its heart. If you wish, throw some Fire of Azrael incense onto the coals (equal parts of cedar, juniper, and sandalwood). This will flare up and burn, but will quickly die down.

With the scented smoke rising from the divinatory incense, scry in the coals. See what shapes the charred wood seem to form, and determine their meaning through the language of symbolism.

BARK DIVINATION

Take a broad, thin piece of bark. Put it into a bright fire until it catches flame, then quickly set it a little distance from the fire.

When it has stopped burning, carefully stare at the symbols visible in the charred and ash-laden wood.

TO CURE

Light a fire of oak wood, if possible. When much of the wood has been reduced to glowing pieces of charcoal, pick up one carefully with a pair of tongs or shovel and throw it immediately into a stream or pot of cold water. It will sizzle and pop. As it does, visualize the disease leaving the body of the afflicted person. Repeat this operation three more times.

TO COMMUNICATE WITH OTHERS

Write a letter to a distant friend as if you were going to mail it. Next, light a blazingly hot fire and throw the letter into it, firmly visualizing the person's face. You should receive a reply.

THE SUN AND GLASS SPELL

Make a drawing of a problem or negative influence in your life on a piece of paper. On a bright, sunny day, take the paper outside with a magnifying glass. Lay the paper on a heat-proof surface and hold the magnifying glass so that its power is concentrated on the center of the paper.

As the paper begins to burn say:

Through glass the sun's bright rays of light
put ill and misfortune to flight.
No more shall you harm me or mine.
Begone! I charge you in this sign.

The problem should clear up.

AN ANTI-FIRE CHARM

To protect your home from the ravages of a devastating fire, place some mistletoe in a blue drawstring bag, douse it thoroughly with cold, clear water, and then immediately hang it in the "heart" of the house—where you and your family spend most of your time.

Or, light a piece of wood and burn to ash. Wet the ashes, let them dry, and hang in a blue drawstring bag. It is done.

8

WATER MAGIC

Water has fascinated us for centuries. It is a vital necessity of life, second only to air, and thus its sacredness rests partially upon this dependence. Water sustains us; therefore, earlier peoples saw it as divine.

Water magic celebrates its mysterious, life-giving nature in a variety of divinations, spells, and rituals. Here are some of them.

Water Gazing

One of the most pleasant, relaxing, and ancient forms of divination is water gazing. Though nearly everyone is familiar with the practice of crystal gazing, few seem to know its ancestor.

There are three basic forms. All use the same technique but different focal points. These are:

1. Gazing into running water, such as that of a stream or brook.

2. Gazing at the shimmering of the sun on the surface of a lake or the ocean.

3. Gazing at the reflections caused by the sun on water, as on the sides of a boat or ship, a nearby structure, or any close object.

It may take a bit of searching to find an ideal place, and in a pinch a swimming pool will substitute for the last form, but once found, the major difficulty is over.

Find a comfortable spot to sit. Relax, still your mind of the thousand thoughts that course through it every waking second. Gently, with eyelids relaxed but not quite closed, gaze into the water, or at the shimmerings of the sun dancing like diamonds, or at the reflections the water casts up of the sun's light.

Allow your thoughts to vanish. If you need an answer to a specific question, once you have attained this drowsy state, formulate the question while still gazing. If no answer immediately comes to mind (and beware the tricks of the conscious mind, which may send wish-fulfilling answers) stop and try again in a few minutes.

If you are inquiring about an absent friend, or a lost article, see that person or object in your mind, let the image dissolve, and see what comes to take its place within your mind's eye.

If, however, you have no special purpose in water gazing, sit quietly and wait until feelings, emotions, symbols, or pictures paint themselves before your eyes, aided by the ever moving, mysterious water.

Though a bit of practice is usually necessary before psychic messages or images are perceived, once attained, you have the art forever.

I have spent hours sitting on a point that juts out into the Pacific Ocean, gazing at the sun's sparkles on the deep blue expanse.

I have also water gazed from the end of piers, on the walls near an outdoor swimming pool, in a fountain in a public park, a puddle in the middle of a sidewalk, even in the bathtub while the sun shone through a window and sent reflections splashing crazily on the tiled walls.

One note of caution: very bright reflections can be damaging to your eyes. If you can't look at the sun's shimmerings for more than a few seconds without blinking, do not attempt water gazing. Wait till the sun's light is softer.

Spring and Well Magic

Have you ever tossed a coin into a well and made a wish? This is a form of water magic that has survived until this age, perhaps because even in these "enlightened" times we are still unconsciously pulled toward the old ways of magic.

Wells have long been associated with femininity and of the great goddess of nature herself, the nurturer. They have surpassed springs in popularity over the years, owing to the newly acquired idea that artificially constructed places are superior in magic to those of earlier "pagan" times. This is a direct result of the growth of political power and social influence that Christianity has enjoyed in Europe from the tenth century until the present.

Many wells have become associated with saints, and healing and other miracles are reputed to have occurred at them. Chalice Well at Glastonbury Abbey in England is an excellent example of an old magical spring that has been transformed into a "well" through the work of early Christian mystics.

But springs have been used in magic much longer than wells. A spring bubbling mysteriously from the earth has long been a source of awe. Not only is it a valuable source of life-giving substance, it is also a natural place to perform magic of all types, such as the following spell:

A SPRING SPELL

Take a small stone from a nearby spring. Upon its surface, using the juice of a local plant or chalk, mark your need in pictures, symbols, or runes (for the latter see appendix II).

Hold the stone in your power hand and walk three times around the spring clockwise. If this isn't possible due to the spring's location, walk in a circle before it three times, moving clockwise.

Lift the stone in your power hand and, staring directly into the heart of the spring, say the following:

Spring of clear water, ceaseless and true,
send me the wish that I now ask of you.

Close your eyes and let the stone drop into the spring. Take a sip of the water. This seals the spell. Leave a token thanks to its spirit.

If nothing happens for three full moons, repeat the spell.

Pond Magic

A gentle, slow-moving pond or lake is an ideal place to perform magical divinations:

RINGS OF WATER

Find a smooth, round pebble or rock. Ask a yes or no question and throw the pebble into the pond. Count the rings that form. If the ripples are of an odd number, the answer is yes. If even, the answer is no.

Stream Magic

Streams, the veins and arteries of the earth, have long been employed in spells, generally to remove something that is negatively affecting the magical practitioner, to cleanse, or to heal. This is clearly evident in the following spells:

A HEALING

When you are sick, find a clear, clean, flowing shallow stream. Remove your clothing (wear a bathing suit if desired) and walk into the stream. Crouch down until the water covers your entire body. If your problem is in your head, duck down under the water for a few seconds before beginning the next part of the spell.

Feel the coolness of the water against your skin; feel it cleansing you, washing away dirt, grit, and disease. Begin chanting in a soft voice the following words, visualizing the sickness as "black worms" wriggling out of your body, into the water of the river, and flowing away from you to the primeval sea, where it will be cleansed.

The sickness is flowing out of me,
into the river, down to the sea.

Repeat the chant for several minutes until you feel like stopping.

Leave the water, dry your body, and it is done.

Naturally, this should not be attempted in a dangerously swift river, if you are too sick to move, or in the place of qualified medical attention. But it can be an aid to the healing processes of the body.

SHIP OF ILLS

Find a small piece of wood—one that will float—and take it to a river. With a knife, carve into the stick all your problems; you can use words, pictures, or symbols. Be sure every problem you can think of is written or depicted on the stick.

If you wish, you can use a pen to write the words but this won't work as well.

While you are doing this, infuse the wood with all your troubles, problems, sorrows, and so on. When you are finished, set it afloat on the water and turn around. Do not look back at the ship of ills as you leave.

Return home, confident that it will travel down the river and on its journey release your problems, one by one, into the water, the great cleanser.

If you wish, you may add a small mast and sail to help it on its way.

Other Water Magic

The following spells, many of which can be performed inside the home, utilize the magic of water in all the classical ways.

FLOWERS AND WATER DIVINATION

This spell, derived from an ancient Greek practice, requires a large bowl or basin, preferably round, about twelve inches across and three or four inches deep. Also necessary is plain water and several small, fresh flowers, each different from the rest in color, appearance, and so on, so that they can be recognized.

This spell is used to determine the course of action to be taken when several different avenues are open to you.

Take the bowl filled with water and the flowers outside and place on a table or on the ground. Sit before it. Taking up one of the flowers, name it for one of your choices (for instance, "sell," or "buy," or "wait") and place it on the water against the far rim of the bowl.

Repeat this process for every choice facing you. When all the flowers are named (remember to recall which represents what) sit quietly before the bowl, whistling aimlessly, without tune, thinking of your dilemma.

The wind should move one of the flowers (or it may seem to move without aid) in your direction. This represents the avenue to be taken.

If none of the flowers move immediately, there may be no answer to your question. Don't fret. Leave the bowl and flowers where they are for a few hours, or overnight, if you wish. Look at it later; one of the flowers will surely have moved by then, and by judging its position from where you sat, you should have an answer.

If two or three flowers have moved, use the closest to your original position before the bowl to determine the answer. If one or more of the flowers have disappeared, it is obvious they weren't the correct choice.

THE CAULDRON AND KNIFE

Just before going to sleep, fill a cauldron (or an old iron bucket, bowl, or pot) with water and place it inside near the front door of the house. Taking a razor-sharp knife, place it point downward into the water, saying as you do:

> Into the water I place this blade
> to guard against the thief and shade.
> May no flesh nor astral shell
> enter this place wherein I dwell.

This is an excellent protection spell, and should be performed every evening before retiring. In the morning remove the knife, wipe the blade dry, and store it in a safe place.

Without touching it, pour the water outside (or down the drain, if necessary) and put the cauldron or bucket away.

Needless to say, do not perform this spell if you expect someone to arrive during the night. Their entrance to your home would be dangerous and spectacularly wet.

This can be done before every door, if desired, and protects against more than human flesh.

THE SACRED LAKE

Lakes are sometimes known as Diana's mirrors. On the night of the full moon, catch its reflection on the still black waters of the lake. Lie down and stare at the reflection, using the same technique as that of water gazing. You should begin to see symbols or even receive psychic messages. It is traditional to call upon Diana, goddess of the moon, while performing this work.

CROSSING WATER

If you are ever out walking or driving and feel danger or "evil" nearby, try to cross over water. This can mean driving over a bridge or stepping over the water running down a gutter or stream. Evil and danger cannot cross over water, for it purifies and neutralizes it, thus rendering you safe.

This is an ancient custom, but can still be used today with good effect.

A MONEY SPELL

Take a dish of water into the moonlight, catch the moon's reflection on the water, and dip your hands into the water. Leave this on the hands until they dry and you shall receive money from an unexpected source within twenty-eight days. This spell should be performed during the waxing moon.

Another version of the same can be done at any time, even when the moon isn't visible. Take a vessel (preferably of silver) to a dark place. Toss a silver coin or piece of silver jewelry into the water and moisten your hands with this.

HEALING WATER

Take a holed stone (see chapter 11: Sea Magic) and put it into a vessel of clear water. Remove it and the water is possessed of healing vibrations that can be used in healing baths, to anoint healing charms, and so on.

A WATER MIRROR

Take a bowl of water and upon its surface let fall a drop of heavy oil. Gaze at the drop of oil as you would a crystal ball and scry.

A HEALING BATH

This is a more convenient version of the river healing technique outlined earlier.

Take a lit silver or white candle, some salt, and a healing oil (such as carnation, violet, sandalwood, or narcissus) into the bathroom.

By the candle's light, run a tub of very warm water. Cast some salt into it, add a few drops of healing oil, and then step into the tub.

Relax. Feel the warm salted water sinking into your pores, through your skin, sterilizing the sick portions of your body.

Visualize the "black worms" leaving it, if you wish, and when you feel the water teeming with them, pull the plug and let the water drain out. While it is draining chant as mentioned previously, with one minor change in wording:

The sickness is flowing out of me,
into the water, down to the sea.

Only when the tub is completely drained stand up. It is best to immediately splash your body with fresh water (a shower is ideal) to remove the last vestiges of the disease of sickness-laden water.

Repeat as needed to speed your body's recovery.

Part III

NATURAL
MAGIC

9

STONE MAGIC

The magic of stones is one that nearly everyone is familiar with, for most people at least know of the existence of birth stones, the stone said to "belong" to the month of your birth. There is also a wide body of lore regarding the powers and magical uses of precious and semiprecious stones. For years it has been commonly said that pearls cause tears, opals are bad luck for some to wear, and that diamonds represent the constancy of love and that is why they are used in wedding and engagement rings.

Though the lore of precious stones and semiprecious stones is often quite contradictory (some authorities claim pearls cause tears of joy, and that opals are good luck) it isn't important, because it is an expensive practice few of us could afford.

But the common, everyday stones you see lying on the street or dig up in your yard, those tumbled up on river banks or beaches, or lying scattered as if a giant hand threw them onto the countryside, are possessed of powers and can be used in magic just as can those of tremendous commercial value.

Simply because a stone is valuable does not lend it any special power. True, the rarer the stone the greater the mystique surrounding it. Diamonds are an excellent example of this. But they are not necessary in magic.

Have you ever idly picked up rocks during a vacation, pocketing pebbles for no apparent reason? Or perhaps you bought a shiny piece of agate or onyx at a gift shop or curio store. Did you ever wonder why?

Hundreds of thousands of years ago rocks were used as tools. They—and bones—were the only tools available, and early peoples used them to collect plants for food, to hunt, sew clothing, and perform any tasks they couldn't accomplish with their bare hands.

Today, rocks aren't thought of too often, unless a gardener finds them in the ground, and curses silently at the work they'll mean to him. But they can be valuable tools in magic, and are cheap and easily obtainable. Live in the city? There must be a park somewhere or a vacant lot.

Rock Meditations

To get in touch with the energies resident within rocks, take a rock that appeals to you. It should be small enough to hold in your hand, but that is the only criteria.

Place it in your power hand and sit quietly. Close your eyes and direct your consciousness to your hand. Feel the rock. Explore it with your mind, noticing the textures and temperature, hardness, and any pieces of dirt clinging to it.

When you have done this, hold the rock passively and let it "speak" to you. It will do this through vibrations, the essence of all magic. The vibrations will come from within the rock itself, and you should feel them in your hand, pounding not only against the palm, but the fingers and thumb as well.

If the vibrations are fast-paced and vigorous, it is a "high-vibration" rock; that is, it is possessed of vibrations that are quickly dispersed and that will act swiftly in any spell in which you might use it.

If the vibrations or pulses are slow and sedate, it is a "low-vibration" stone and its uses will be different.

This should be done with every rock you intend to utilize in magic. Though it may sound like a long procedure, it is actually quite short. Once you know the vibrations, it can be done in a matter of seconds.

These are some of the ways these stones may be used:

Divining Stones

This is a simple device used to obtain yes or no answers to pertinent questions. As such, it is a form of divination.

Stones have existed for a long time and will be around for quite a bit longer. As such, they are symbols of the wisdom of eternity. They are frequently turned to for answers to important questions.

Obtain three stones. One, of a bright color, should be a high-vibration stone. Another, of a dark color, should possess low vibrations. Select a third that seems to have medium vibrations that are neither high nor low. This should be unusually colored so that it can be easily differentiated from the others. All three stones, in fact, should be of such individual appearances that they are immediately recognizable.

When you need an answer to a yes/no question, roll the stones in your hands like dice, mentally asking your question, then throw them onto a flat surface, preferably the ground. A table will do.

When the stones have stopped, determine the answer by their positions. If the "yes" stone is closer to the indicator, that is the answer. The same with the "no" stone. If the stones are equally apart there is no answer.

This simple method can be highly accurate, and I have used it for years with good results.

The stones should be kept in a small bag of their own in a protected place and used for no other purposes.

With practice, a more definitive answer can be determined. The positions of the stones, their proximity to the diviner, and the questions asked can all be taken into consideration. The closer the stones are to the indicator the stronger the answer.

Practice and experience will allow you greater accuracy with the divining stones.

Talking Stones

In this technique, stones are struck with knives to produce sound. If the right stone and the right knife are brought together, the sound will be musical and, if repeated, can be used to induce a trancelike state.

High-vibration stones are best for this. The technique is simple: hold the stone and strike it gently with a knife blade. Have a wide variety of knives and stones (be careful of the knives—they should be dull for this use).

After you have experimented for a while, select the combination producing the best sound. In a candle-lit room or on a wind-swept hill or anywhere, of course, strike the rock and listen to the sound.

Repeat in any rhythm you like. Just like the medicine man's drum or rattle, the sounds and rhythms will work to put you into a relaxed, drowsy state. At this time you can perform divinations, meditation or simply experience the moment and sensations.

This should be done out of sight (and hearing) of others. At night beneath a full moon is extremely powerful, and may suggest other uses.

The same technique may be used with gongs or bells, but that is outside our area of interest.

TO COMMUNICATE WITH OTHERS AT LONG DISTANCES

On a high-vibration stone, mark your message with chalk or charcoal. Bury it deep in the earth while visualizing the person's face, and your message will be sent.

A PROTECTIVE STONE

Take a small high-vibration stone and hold it in your power hand. For several minutes, preferably sitting on the bare earth, chant the following in a low voice, all the while staring at the stone:

Stone, evil you shall deny,
send it to the earth and sky.
Send it to the flame and sea.
Stone of power, protect me.

Now carry the stone with you at all times as a good-luck charm. It will not only absorb your own vibrations, thus making it uniquely yours, it will also release its own energies to form a kind of protective barrier surrounding you, a shield of protective power to get you through the day unharmed.

A CIRCLE OF STONES

If you wish to charge or otherwise infuse with energy any object, such as a ring, piece of jewelry, and so on, take a handful of high-vibration stones of an odd number and form a ring with them on a table, the floor or, best of all, on the ground. The latter is also the most difficult, for they must be in a place where they can stay put for at least a day. The table-top method is easier.

Once the stones have been situated, place the object to be charged within them in the very center of the circle.

This is all you have to do, for the stones will work their magic, sending strong vibrations into the object. If you wish to strengthen the power of the spell, draw the appropriate rune (see appendix II) on each stone before forming the ring. This will enable you to imbue the object with specific energies.

An example would be a ring you are about to give to a loved one. The runes of "love" and "protection" could be placed upon the stones, to ensure that the receiver is indeed suffused with love and protection.

POT OF STONES

Fill an old pot or jar with low-vibration stones. Place this pot in a hidden spot in your home where it will never be disturbed.

The stones will spread their low energy throughout the area, spreading peace and calm as well.

Your household should be happy and free of major problems and upsets.

THE BAG OF SEVEN STONES

This spell requires seven stones, of either high or low vibrations. You should have one each of these colors: white, green, red, orange, yellow, brown, and black.

It is best if you can find all of these stones yourself. Stream beds are excellent places to look. If you have difficulty, go ahead and buy them.

Place the stones in a sack made of a natural cloth dyed yellow—cotton is excellent. When you desire a sneak peek into the future, hold the bag, reach inside without looking, and remove one of the stones. The stone reveals present or future conditions:

WHITE: peace, tranquility

GREEN: love, money

RED: passion, arguments

ORANGE: luck

YELLOW: wisdom, lessons

BROWN: objects, possessions, gifts

BLACK: negativity

10

TREE MAGIC

Trees have from time immemorial been closely associated with magic. These stout members of the vegetable kingdom may stand for as long as a thousand years, and tower far above our mortal heads. As such, they are symbols and keepers of unlimited power, longevity, and timelessness.

An untouched forest, studded with trees of all ages, sizes, and types, is more than a mysterious, magical place—it is one of the energy reservoirs of nature. Within its boundaries stand ancient and new sentinels, guardians of the universal force that has manifested on the earth in vegetable form.

As such, a forest is an excellent spot for magical workings of any kind, not only tree magic. But any tree, anywhere in the world, can be used for the spells and techniques discussed here. Since each type of tree has its own particular powers, these will be outlined after the actual techniques are presented.

Bear in mind that tree magic needn't be limited to these tree types, for every tree has its own inherent powers that vary from tree to tree. Experiment!

All trees, save for the poisonous ones (such as yew and hemlock) are excellent for healing magic. Any tree can be used to take away a headache and give you energy, or to reveal the future. We are limited purely by our own minds and actions.

It is important to talk to any tree(s) you are working magic with. Tell them exactly what your need is. Explain to them why the need exists and its urgency. Trees are living entities with a consciousness that, while different from our own, is still capable of communication upon subtler planes of awareness.

So, even though old spells sometimes direct you to pound nails into trees—please don't. This is not only damaging and hurtful to the tree, it is absolutely unnecessary, for there are other techniques available.

Some of these spells require marking symbols on leaves. A stick that has been burned on one end is excellent, for the charcoal will act as the graphite in a pencil. Practice with this until you become proficient.

A TREE SPELL

When you have found a tree to work magic with, take a large leaf, a charcoal-tipped stick, a piece of flexible vine or natural-fiber cord, and a dime to the tree.

Sitting beneath it, write or draw a symbol of your need with the stick.

Rise and walk nine times around the tree clockwise, saying the following or similar words:

Ancient one of the ancient earth,
older than time can tell,

grant me the power at your command
to charge my magic spell.

Repeat as often as necessary until you have walked nine times around the tree.

When finished, tie the leaf around the trunk as tightly as you can with the vine. If this isn't possible, find a branch and tie it on there.

When you are sure that the leaf is secure, take the dime and bury it at the foot of the tree in the earth in payment for its help. Now leave the area and let the tree do its work.

If, when you return to the tree, the leaf is gone—don't worry. The forces have already been set in motion.

Tree Healing Spells

Though the above spell can be used with any sort of magical need, trees have long been looked to for aid in healing, so here are several formulas that can be used.

TO CURE

Tie a red string around the patient's neck, just before he or she retires for the night. In the morning, immediately untie the string and retie it around a tree trunk or branch, thereby transferring the sickness to the tree. The tree will send it down into the earth. Be sure to leave an offering of thanks at the base of the tree.

A HEALING

Find a strong, particularly healthy and vibrant tree, one with slim, flexible branches. When you are sick, go to the tree and tie a knot gently in one of the branches or twigs. This must not hurt the tree, so make the knot loose but tight enough to retain its shape.

Ask the tree for its help in healing you. "Pour" the disease or wound into the knot, visualizing it in detail for several minutes.

Then untie the knot, again with care so that the tree isn't damaged. This will release the disease and it will sink into the earth. Bury an offering at the tree's base.

TO CURE BACKACHE

Circle the tree nine times clockwise, asking it to ease your pain, using a chant such as this one:

> **O great tree, O strong tree,**
> **absorb my pain so I'll be free.**

Lie back against the tree's firm, solid trunk; press your back into the bark. Feel the tree absorbing the pain and your back releasing it into the tree.

After a few minutes, rise and thank the tree by burying something precious at its foot.

TO BREAK A BAD HABIT

Make a picture of yourself or the bad habit on a leaf or piece of bark. Take it to a proper tree and bury it at its roots. Place an offering to the tree in the hole with the leaf or bark and cover it up. Pour some water onto the spot and it is done.

TO REGAIN LOST ENERGY

Sit with your back pressed against the tree trunk and let the tree's limitless energy flow into you. Very excellent if you have been walking or hiking long distances.

TO DIVINE THE FUTURE

Lie beneath leafy trees and relax, gazing up into the ever-shifting canopy of green above you. Watch the random patterns formed by the wind's gentle lifting and pushing of the leaves. This should lull you to a state where you open up psychically and receive messages concerning questions you have.

A TREE LOVE SPELL

On a small leaf make an image of yourself. On another make an image of the type of person you wish to meet. With a green thread, sew the two images together face to face and knot the string tightly.

Go to a tree that emits loving vibrations and find a natural crevice or hole in the tree (don't make one). If none is available, perhaps the place where a branch is joined to the trunk can be used as long as it is secure.

Lodge the leaves firmly into the crevice and say as you do:

Tree of earth, water, air, and fire,
grant me the love that I desire.

Bury seven pennies at its base and it is done.

The trees with which you cultivate magical relationships are things to be treasured; visit them often, even when you have no magic to perform. When you can arrive at the point when you accept the trees as friends, you have achieved a powerful bond between yourself, the earth, and even beyond.

The Magical Powers of Trees

ALMOND: divination, clairvoyance, money, loans, business

APPLE: healing, prosperity, love, perpetual youth

ASH: protection, sea magic (when performing those spells far from any ocean. See chapter 17: Sea Magic)

APRICOT: love

ASPEN: protection

BIRCH: protection, purification, fertility, new beginnings

CEDAR: prosperity, longevity

COCONUT: purity, chastity, healing

CYPRESS: past-life workings, protection

ELDER: healing, protection, prosperity

ELM: protection

EUCALYPTUS: healing

FIG: fertility, strength, energy, health

HAWTHORN: cleansing, marriage, love, protection

HAZEL: divination, marriage, protection, reconciliation

HEMLOCK: not recommended for use

JUNIPER: protection

LEMON: divination, healing, chastity, neutrality

LIME: divination, healing, chastity, neutrality

LINDEN: protection

MAPLE: divination, love

MULBERRY: knowledge, divination, wisdom, the will

OAK: healing, strength, money, longevity

OLIVE: peace, fruitfulness, security, money, marriage, fidelity

ORANGE: love, marriage

PALM: strength, wisdom

PEACH: love, divination

PINE: purification, health, fortune, prosperity, fertility

ROWAN: protection, strength

WALNUT: healing, protection

WILLOW: healing, protection, enchantments, easy delivery
of babies, wishing

YEW: not recommended for use

11

IMAGE MAGIC

Image magic usually conjures up visions of sneering voodoo dolls bristling with black-headed pins. We have the media and a century of fundamentalist propaganda to thank for that.

The so-called voodoo doll, which is neither solely connected with that much-misunderstood religion, nor is necessarily a doll, has as its roots image magic, which has been known in every magical system since the dawn of recorded history.

Everywhere, images have been made of various types of wood, clay, lead, gold, and silver. They have been marked on large leaves, bark, animal skins, and fashioned from lemons, onions, apples, eggs, turnips, nuts, coconuts, limes, potatoes, and the infamous mandrake root.

Sometimes the image is carved to the minutest detail, right down to the strands of hair. At other times it is a crude outline engraved onto flat surfaces such as peels of fruits, bark, or even in the earth herself, scratched with fingernails or sticks into the dust.

Whatever the substances, whatever the spell, the image stands as one of the most-used objects in the history of magic.

Today, after nearly five thousand years of continuous use as a technique, it has a wholly unfounded evil reputation.

True, image magic has been used for negative purposes, but so has nearly every other form of magic. Its most useful contribution to the magical arts is that it enables us to have a plan or diagram for ourselves or those we're working magic for.

Not that the image actually becomes the person represented; no images are baptized or breathed into life, as in some of the darker workings.

The outlines or images simply serve as blueprints with which we plan and make our future selves, always in improved conditions.

Books of magic that crowd the shelves of occult stores today are full of image magic, usually designed to cause torture or death, and the dolls themselves can usually be purchased, through the mail, complete with pins!

But none of this will be discussed here. Instead, the more humane aspects will be explored, and the spells—all of which are easy—are those that vibrate love and healing, protection and blessing.

While it is commonly supposed that image magic is performed with dolls, figure candles, or paper cutouts, the first three spells given here are best performed with a flat dish of moist earth that you have freshly gathered. Before using the earth, remove any rocks, twigs, and other impurities.

Spread the moist earth or sand an inch deep in a round dish or plate—preferably at least ten inches in diameter to give you plenty of room.

This will be your "canvas" upon which you will mark your image.

Your writing instrument will be a sturdy twig, or perhaps a sharpened pencil. Thousands of years ago they used stylus and clay.

If the earth is too dry, you may wish to add a little water. If you cannot obtain clean soil, then collect some sand (or buy some) and wet it until it "sets," that is, until it will retain a figure sketched onto the sand.

These preparations are to be repeated for each piece of image magic you do. Return the used dirt after a spell to the earth.

Of course, if you can actually perform these spells on the ground, results will be better, since this is the way they were originally done. The spells will have to be modified slightly, but again, it will be well worth the effort.

A BASIC IMAGE SPELL

Fill container with clean, moist earth. With a writing instrument (a stick, twig, or pencil) draw an outline of yourself on the earth. Make the image facing you and be sure to contour the lines as closely as possible with your own body; the bulges and flat parts, the proportions of legs to torso, and the shape of the head and hair.

Add no distinguishing features to the outline; they are unnecessary. If your first effort doesn't satisfy you, smooth it out with your fingers and start another.

When you are pleased with the outline, stop, and with the writing instrument, draw squarely over the image—directly on top of it—a symbol representing your need.

Make this symbol as real and perfect as you can. If you are satisfied with the results, put the writing instrument away and sit in quiet contemplation of the image. The symbol covering your outline represents the need manifesting in your life.

After a few minutes, walk away from the image and clear your mind of thoughts about the spell.

If necessary, put the vessel of earth carefully out of sight, making sure not to disturb the image therein. Twice a day, every morning and night, gaze at the picture for a few minutes.

After a week pour the soil back onto the earth. What shall be, shall be.

TO BE FREE OF SOMETHING NEGATIVE

Draw an outline of yourself in the soil. Next, over it, draw a symbol representing that which you wish to be free of.

Draw this symbol over the image. Gaze at it, see the symbol as part of yourself, as you are now.

Then, with careful strokes, completely erase the symbol with your fingertips. Make sure you don't damage your original outline, however, if this happens, redraw immediately.

Now gaze at the new you, free of the negative aspect and ready to start again with a cleaner slate.

Repeat every day for seven days.

A DIETING SPELL

Draw an outline of the figure you desire. Make it perfect in every way (you may wish to draw this in profile to mark the correct proportions).

Next, draw an outline of yourself as you are now around the perfect you.

Set it aside in a safe place until the full moon.

On this night take the image out from its hiding place and with your finger smooth down a tiny portion of the larger outline. In effect, you are symbolically removing this weight from your figure.

Repeat this every day for fourteen days while the moon wanes. On the fourteenth day, you should have erased the current you and have left only the perfected you.

In this time, of course, you will have been eating properly and exercising. Magic requires physical support.

If the spell doesn't work this fast (and it generally doesn't), start over again at the next full moon. Persevere, try, and you shall succeed.

APPLE IMAGES

Image magic often employs apples. With a sharp knife, carve in the peel of a red apple a picture of your need. Expose the yellowish-white flesh behind the peel with your carving so that the symbol is clearly visible. This may take some practice.

Now, after gazing at the symbol for a few minutes, eat the apple down to the core. Save the seeds and plant them, if you wish. As the symbol has become part of you physically, so too shall what it represents.

This can be used to bring anything to you.

IMAGE MAGIC FOR OTHERS

Remember: magic should be done for others only when they have asked for it, or agreed to it.

If there is something that a friend needs desperately, make an image of it. Any material can be used, from sheets of silver to pen and ink to knitting and crocheting. Make the image as perfectly as you can, then give it to them, so that the real object (or quality) it represents may be drawn into their lives.

If someone you know is sick and they request your magical help, make an image of them using green or blue cloth. If you are no expert at sewing, you still should be able to cut out two crude human outlines and stitch them together.

Just before they are completely sewn together, stuff the image with healing herbs, such as those listed in appendix III. Then stitch the image shut.

Place it gently between two blue candles. Light the candles and, if possible, burn a healing incense (one can be made of cinnamon, rosebuds, and myrrh) in a censer placed behind the image.

All the while during the construction of the doll, concentrate on the person as being fully healed, alive, well, back to normal.

Do not see the disease or wound; do not think of it at all. Banish all thoughts of it from your mind; see the person as whole and well again.

When the image is completed, and it is lying between the candles, with the incense smoke twisting up behind it, say the following, or any heart-felt plea:

I have fashioned this image,
which is the perfect image of . . . (name) . . .
who was struck down and harmed by
. . . (name of disease or problem) . . .
I know that the earth can help heal him/her,
just as she heals the wounded bird and

the gasping fish.
All-powerful Mother Earth,
you who controls all,
heal . . . (name) . . . of that which cannot be healed in
    any other way.

Any impassioned plea will be heard, to any deity. After a few minutes, quench the candles and put everything carefully away.

Repeat the process the usual seven days in a row, placing the image between the candles and saying the above, or similar, words. If no promising results come immediately, take the old one carefully apart, scatter the herbs, bury all in the earth, and make a new image. Work with this precisely as you did the last one.

Such spells, of course, should be used only in conjunction with orthodox healing methods, or when such methods have failed.

AN IMAGE LOVE CHARM

This and similar image spells are most popular today, as they have been for ages.

Carve, sew, or otherwise construct an image of yourself at your finest, physically speaking. Pour into it all your good points, as well as your bad. Embody the image with your spirit, your life-force, your total being. When you look at its face (however crude or unfinished it may seem to be) see your own face.

When finished, put in a safe place. Next, of the same material, fashion an image of your ideal love. This shouldn't be a specific person, of course, but a composite of everything you are looking for in a man or woman. Though you are only fashioning its outline or rough features, implant in it physical, spiritual, emotional, intellectual, and other qualities; habits and goals in life; any particulars that appeal or are important to you.

When both images are finished, take a pink or red thread or cord and tie them loosely together. Place them in a spot where they will not be disturbed for several weeks, but not in a box or other constricting place. Someone will come to you, and after that, it will be up to the two of you.

Spells of this nature draw many people to you, and one or two of these might become good friends. A more personal relationship might develop out of one of these, which may eventually lead to love.

If it does but the relationship ends, unbind the images, carefully dismantle the one of the perfect love, and begin anew.

The same is true if you find no lover, but for this wait at least three months.

A spell of this type doesn't force the person you meet to fall in love with you; it simply expands your circle of friends. Any person you meet will be under no magical pressure or force to love you; that you will have to do on your own.

12

KNOT MAGIC

The magic of knots stretches back at least four thousand years, when cuneiform tablets were produced in the Near East describing various types of magic involving the use of knots.

Despite the fact that it has been known in most every culture and most probably in every age, knot magic is falling into disuse today and is in danger of being completely forgotten.

Why would a worldwide, simple, practical, and effective form of magic be forgotten? Probably for the very fact that it is simple and practical. Too often, magic has been elaborated with ritual to the point of absurdity; something easy was looked upon suspiciously by those who were taught pageantry and stylized ritual.

Knot magic is still as powerful today as it was in 2000 BCE, and is still being worked with good results today.

There are many "survivals" of knot magic in contemporary culture. In folklore, "survival," is when a custom or superstition is practiced or remembered by people who have forgotten its origins.

Why do we tie a string around a finger to remember something important, for instance? Just what is meant by the saying "he's bound to do it"?

The act of tying a knot brings into concrete, physical form an abstract idea, concept, or thought. Thus, when you tie a knot around your finger while thinking of the thing you wish to remember, you are making a connection in your mind between the knot (the physical) and the thought you need to remember (the mental). On a more magical level, you tie the knot not to remind you of the subject, but to ensure that you do remember it.

One of the techniques of knot magic is to tie a knot especially around an image of a person, literally "binding" the image with a cord, or the image to an object, with the intention of inhibiting the person's actions, thoughts, and so on. "He's bound to do it" harks back to a time when this was literally believed— someone would do something because his or her image had been bound.

Sound far-fetched? Several hundred years ago there were many laws and statutes against binding images, or of knot work in magic.

In fact, at one time, any ornaments twisted, knotted, or plaited were considered heathen and idolatrous in Germany, while magical knots, on the other hand, were frequently carved into churches to guard against the entry of pagan magic or "spirits."

The history of knot magic is indeed long and fascinating, but the basic techniques are still more interesting. They are presented here, but a reminder is perhaps necessary.

The actions you perform during a spell or work of magic aren't as important as the need behind them. You must send out your own energy (through your emotion) toward your need or the magic will be fruitless.

Magic isn't the empty parroting of words and actions; it is an involved, emotionally charged experience in which the words and actions are used as focal points or keys to unlock the power that we all possess.

The Cords

Knot magic is generally performed with cords. These can be of any color, but there are specific associations with colors and these are listed in appendix I.

Cords should be of natural materials, such as wool—the best—or cotton. Avoid stiff, tightly woven, rough, or plastic-based cords, like those of nylon, rayon, or polyester.

For most spells you won't need more than a foot or two of cord; however, if there are several knots involved, use plenty of cord, for knots "eat up" a great deal of length.

Keep your magical cords out of plain sight, so that they won't be used for other things and won't, therefore, be infused with other vibrations.

If you wish to braid, weave, or spin your own cords they will be much more powerful, for they are of your own hands and you can concentrate on your need during their construction. Braiding is, in itself, a magical act.

A SIMPLE KNOT SPELL

Take a cord of any color, provided it is pleasing to you and, preferably, is made of a natural fiber. Firmly visualize your need; take the cord, build up as much emotion as you can, then all at once tie a firm knot in the cord.

Pull on the ends of the cord until they are taut; this releases the power to go and do your bidding.

The power isn't inside the knot; it is released to draw your need into manifestation. The knotted cord is a physical representation of your need, just as an image is. Until it arrives, keep the cord with you or somewhere safe in your house.

Ensure that the knot doesn't come untied. If this does happen, start another knot spell.

When your need has manifested in the physical (always, of course, in a natural way—a diamond necklace or tickets for a trip around the world won't drop into your lap five seconds after you cast a spell for wealth or travel) you can do one of several things with the cord.

You can burn it, to ensure that it will never come unknotted, or bury it, where it will disintegrate, or leave it safely in a box or chest where it won't be touched.

This spell can be used with any need. If you ever wish to undo or reverse the spell, take the cord and untie the knot. This doesn't always work, however, so be warned.

If you've burned or buried the cord, you won't be able to reverse the spell. But this doesn't matter, really, for if your need truly is a need, time won't alter it, and ten years from now, I doubt you'll look back and wish to reverse a spell!

I included the above information strictly because it is traditional.

A DESTRUCTIVE KNOT SPELL

If there is a situation, problem, or possible menace you are facing, there is a knot spell for this. Take the cord and firmly visualize the problem in all its agonizing detail. Become emotional about it; seethe with anger, crumble into tears, whatever works. Then firmly tie the knot.

Walk away from it—out of the room—if possible. Take a shower, eat, do whatever will get your mind off the spell and allow you to relax.

When your emotions are stabilized, return to the knot. With calm and peace, untie the knot. See the problem vanishing; dissolving into a dust that is swept away by the cleansing, refreshing north wind.

It is done.

BINDING OBJECTS

Binding is a practical example of how this usually harmful (and therefore strictly "hands-off") form of magic can be an effective and perfectly harmless magical procedure.

If a friend wants to borrow something, and you feel hesitant in letting the object out of your hands, but you must, take the object (if it's something small enough to move around and hold), and a cord.

Bind the object to your body—literally—physically tie the object to yourself. Stand or sit a few minutes, visualizing yourself receiving the object back from the person you're loaning it to.

Afterward, cut the cord (do not untie the knot!) and loan the object out, assured you'll once more have it in your possession.

If the object is too large, such as a car, take a piece of cord, tie your hand or arm to a piece of it (such as the steering wheel, antenna, and so on), and proceed as above.

Put the cord in a safe place until the object returns.

A LOVE SPELL

Take three cords or strings of various, pleasing pastel colors, perhaps pink, red, and green, and braid them tightly together. Firmly tie a knot near one end of the braid, thinking of your need for love.

Next, tie another knot, and another, until you have tied seven knots. Wear or carry the cord with you until you find your love.

After that, keep the cord in a safe place, or give to one of the elements—scatter and burn the ashes in the ocean or a stream.

A LOVE BINDING

This one is rather sneaky, but it should only be used when a relationship has been established. It is to give a little boost to the love for both parties involved.

Take a garment, small and flexible, that belongs to your beloved—one that won't be easily missed. Take one of your own garments and tie them together firmly. Hide these where they won't be found.

This can help you stay together happily.

A HEALING

Tie nine knots in a piece of red thread and wear around the neck to help cure ills and diseases. This is especially good for headaches.

ANOTHER HEALING

Bind the sick one (or yourself) with red cord. Then, untie the knot and throw the cord onto a blazing fire, saying:

I put the disease upon the fire; let it consume away as
the cord consumes; let it vanish as the smoke!

As it burns, visualize the disease doing just that.

A PROTECTIVE BINDING

Take a cord and tie nine knots in it, visualizing a shield, a flaming sword, a latched hook, a firearm; whatever you associate
with protection against hostility, outside forces, or physical vi-
olence. Hang up the cord in your home or carry with you for
personal protection.

AN EGYPTIAN KNOT AMULET

In a long cord, tie seven knots and then a square knot to join
the ends. Carry for protection.

TO AID CURING ANYTHING

Tie a cord that has nine knots in it firmly around the part of
the body affected. Untie the knot, then the nine in the cord,
and throw it into running water.

A WISHING LADDER

Obtain a long piece of cord of the color that corresponds to
your need. Also obtain nine seeds, nuts, pieces of bark, dried
flowers, or sprigs of herbs that are magically related to your
need. (See Chapter 10 or appendix III.)

Take a bit of the herb and tie a knot around it with the cord,
pulling it taut, firmly visualizing your need.

Repeat this process eight more times until the cord is studded with nine knots, each of which holds a piece of bark or a flower.

Next, take the cord outside, hold it up to the sky, and say:

Ladder of knots that numbers nine,
I've fashioned you to draw me
the need that I wish would be mine.
This is my will, so mote it be!

Hang up the wishing ladder in a place of importance in the home, or place it coiled around a candlestick in which you've placed a candle of the appropriate color.

Not only are wishing ladders magically effective, they are also highly decorative.

Some Knot Magic Notes

Unfortunately, the vast majority of knot spells that have survived until this age are negative ones. While of historical interest, such knot spells have no place in a discussion of this nature, for such magic is not divine and will indeed lead to its worker's destruction.

There are, however, some other processes and tidbits of knot lore that are highly appropriate.

It is best when performing magic of any kind to have the hair loose and unbraided, if long. The symbolism is obvious: the knots or twists might inhibit the power.

When casting a protective spell however, braided or knotted hair, plus crocheted or knitted clothing (sweaters are ideal during the winter) are valuable plusses.

A net, for the same reason, is extremely protective. Many sea Witches and magicians have a net in their homes. Not only does it blend in with the seaside atmosphere, it is also very powerful.

So, too, for that matter, is a macramé hanging.

If you wake and have knots in your hair, it is said that elves and fairies have played in your hair while you slept, thus accounting for the knots. The association of elves and fairies with knots is quite ancient, and harks back to an age when magic was science.

If you ever need to do a knot spell and haven't a cord handy, or can't use one, go through the motions of picking up a piece of cord and knotting it, firmly visualizing your need, just as in a regular knot spell.

It will be just as powerful as a spell you've performed with a physical cord in your hands.

And if you ever wish to ensure that you remember something important, tie a string around your finger!

13

CANDLE MAGIC

The magic of candles is a complex art, and several good books have been written on the subject (see the bibliography). The basics, however, are presented here, since they can be incorporated into other forms of magic. It is also quite a practical method. The few rituals and spells presented here cover a wide variety of situations and may be altered slightly with a dash of creativity to fit any need.

Candleburning magic works with the help of fire (the candle's flame), color (the candle itself), as well as any other agencies you wish to use. Herbs are often utilized in conjunction with candle magic because they are powerhouses in and of themselves.

The Candles

Candles are available in a wide variety of size, shape, and design, as a visit to a good candle shop will attest. When candles are intended for magic, however, the variations increase tenfold. There are figure candles, knobbed candles, skull and mummiform candles, even "devil" and crucifix candles!

Candles are available in every color, from the purest white to the richest black, in size ranging from a toothpick to massive three-foot monsters.

All are fine, all are expensive, and all are unnecessary. Simple tapers—available in grocery stores, hardware shops, and specialty businesses—are fine for use.

Magically speaking, beeswax candles are ideal, for the symbolism of the bee and the fact that the wax itself is a product of nature. Unfortunately, beeswax candles are incredibly expensive, and unless you have hives and candle-making abilities, the cheaper petroleum-based candles will do.

Since each color has different attributes, you will have to match the candle to your need. There are two systems you can follow. Either match the need to one of the elements and use that element's color, or consult the chart in appendix I for the corresponding color.

Either way, make sure your candles are free of cracks or breaks, for these destroy the power of the candles.

When you buy candles for use in magic, try to keep them in a special place where they won't be handled.

Candleholders

These, too, may be purchased from any store. The most important consideration is that the holder keep the candle in an upright position. There must be no possibility that the candle will fall while it is lit, or that when it burns down, it may set the holder on fire. This rules out wooden or plastic holders. Also be wary of holders that transfer heat, like metal ones, as they may scorch surfaces on which they're placed.

Herbs

If you wish to use herbs, choose ones from the lists in appendix II. Though there are no hard and fast rules, a mixture of three or more herbs is more powerful than a single herb. Each ingredient adds its own powers and the mixture is much more beneficial than each of its separate ingredients.

As a rule of thumb, include an odd number of herbs, and be certain that every one relates specifically to your need.

If you cannot find a suitable herb, use rosemary. This herb—a favorite of Italian cooks—is also one of the most-used magical herbs, for its powers can be utilized for nearly every magical need.

A SIMPLE CANDLE SPELL

Take the appropriately colored candle, the holder, and any herbs you are using to a flat surface where you can leave the candle burning for several hours. (If you have an altar or other magical working space, use that.)

Place the candle in a holder then sprinkle pinches of any herbs you are using around the holder or inside it, if there is space. This needn't be more than a light sprinkling, especially if the herbs actually contact the candle itself within the holder; too much might catch fire.

All you have to do now is light the candle. But why not do it in a magical way? Turn off the lights (candle magic is at its best at night, but will work during the day). Take a matchbook, and hold it and the match high, but away from your head.

Strike the match smartly against the book and, as it flames out, lower it until it lights the candle. While you do this, think of a spark of the elemental energy of fire descending to empower your magic.

As the candle's flame glows brighter, throw the match into a heat-proof ashtray (do not blow or shake it out). Sit or stand in quiet visualization of your need as you watch the candle's flame.

The herbs sprinkled around the base of the candle send their energies up in a cone shape. The energies mix with those of the candle's color at the flame, and, from there, spread out in all directions, starting the process of drawing your need to you.

If you wish, you may chant a few words as you light the candle, or state your need aloud, but this isn't really necessary. The flame, color, and herbs will do their work without it.

Leave the candle burning until it is completely consumed, if possible. If not, pinch or snuff the flame out and relight as soon as possible. Never leave burning candles unattended.

This simple ritual can be elaborated on immeasureably. A simple example is the use of runes. The appropriate rune can be carved onto the candle with a knife or drawn on a piece of paper and placed under the holder. Stones may be placed around the candle, particularly suited for protective rituals, and the candles can be annointed with scented oils to add their own vibrations. Since oils have the same magical uses as the plants from which they are extracted, the list of herbs in appendix III is an excellent guide.

Following are a few candle divinations. These represent some of the last vestiges of the age-old practice of consulting fires to determine likely future events, or to gain insight.

A MULTI-CANDLE DIVINATION

Set up as many identical candles in holders as you have choices facing you. If you wish an answer to a simple question, use two candles: one for yes, one for no.

In an area free of breezes, name each candle after one of your choices and light them.

The first to burn down and sputter out is your best bet.

THREE-CANDLE DIVINATION

Set up three candles, all of the same color, in identical holders, if possible, in a windless place. Arrange them in a triangle and light them.

If one burns more brightly than the others, you'll have a period of unexpected good luck. A quenched flame signifies a period of negativity. If the flames move in circles, someone may be working against you. Sparks shooting out are also negative signs. If all the candles burn steadily, undisturbed, and peacefully, your life will be the same.

ONE-CANDLE DIVINATION

Light a candle. Keep it lit for several hours, with no drafts nearby. Ask a yes or no question. Now sit quietly and watch the candle.

If the right side burns faster than the left, the answer is yes. If the reverse, the answer is no.

When burning a candle to determine future influences, the right signifies good fortune. However, if the left side burns more quickly than the right, prospects are ill.

14

WAX MAGIC

Divination through the use of candle wax is an aspect of fire magic that makes use of fire's illuminating qualities to light up the future. The techniques and preparations are simple, and the results surprisingly helpful.

Following are two techniques of candle or wax reading—the drip and molten methods. Both have their benefits and drawbacks.

The candle drip method is the easiest, but the results are often difficult to interpret and much practice is needed to gain accurate readings.

The molten wax usually produces fine results, but you do have to melt the wax first, which can be not only messy but even dangerous, if precautions aren't taken. Since wax, either the preferred beeswax or the petroleum-based, is exorbitantly expensive at the moment, this is another matter to consider. The shape formed by the molten wax, however, is surprisingly easy to read and is therefore well worth the expense.

Here are the two methods.

Candle Drip Divination

For this you will need a number of long tapers (eight inches or longer) of the four basic elemental colors—green, yellow, red, and blue. One of these is necessary for every reading. You will also need a large, round or square vessel filled with cold water. This can be of any material, but pottery or glass are best, for they can withstand heat. Plastic is not recommended.

Put the candles, a book of matches, and the vessel of water on a table or other flat surface. You are now ready to begin wax divination.

If you have a particular question you want answered, use the color candle related to your question, through the symbolism of the elements (see chapter 4: The Elements). If the question doesn't seem to be related to any of the elements, use a white candle.

If you have no question but are simply desiring a glimpse into your own future, use a yellow candle, for this is the color of divination in general.

Light the candle and hold it upright over the water for a moment, thinking about your question or simply calming your mind.

When the candle is fully flaming and has begun melting the wax, tilt it and hold steadily about an inch over the water's surface.

The wax will begin dripping onto the water.

If the tiny drips (which harden into small droplets of wax, smooth on the top but round on the bottom) do not merge and create a pattern, you aren't concentrating on the question. Sweep everything else from your mind.

The wax drops will form a pattern on the surface of the water.

If you have trouble achieving this, begin moving the candle slowly, allowing the drops to touch one another and so form a line on the water. If this is done for a few minutes, a definite shape will appear on the water.

When this happens, quench the candle's flame with your fingers or a candle snuffer and set aside. Look at the shape. What does it look like? Pick it up carefully so as not to break it and turn it over. Does it look the same, or different? Study its thickness to see if it says anything to you symbolically.

Here are some shapes and patterns commonly found in the drip method and their traditional meanings. As you can see, this form of divination is rather limited.

Spirals

The most common, because of the way the wax rotates on the surface of the water, spirals represent reincarnation, the universe, the world, or perhaps a particular life. It could be you need to evolve beyond it, or that it is something from a previous life. Perhaps, depending on the nature of the question, the problem (or its solution) is in the home. This is an excellent example of how interpretation must be a personal thing; no one else can tell you exactly how these symbols relate to you. Usually, the first meaning that comes into your mind is the correct one.

Circles

Circles represent eternity and fertility, and both of these attributes can be interpreted according to the question asked. Fertility would perhaps represent a new activity, financial security, or even a new baby on the way! It may also signify the successful completion of a project. Eternity may mean just that—it will be a long time before something is completed or comes to pass. Circles also represent religion and spirituality, and thus can be seen in this context during interpretation.

Broken Lines

If the wax drops form into lines but they aren't connected, it represents a scattering of forces, or a lack of focus in your life, business, or other pursuits. It can also signify forces working against you, but don't take this too literally—such forces may well be within your own being. This isn't a positive pattern to find, for it is a sign that changes must be made to bring order into your life.

Dots

Unconnected wax drops are sometimes the only thing you can get. As stated before, this sometimes signifies lack of attention on the divination, but it can also mean that the problem is too complex for an answer at this time. If you try wax divination several times with only dots coming up each time, you're either asking the wrong questions or, if you haven't asked one, you shouldn't be seeking a glimpse into the future at this time—at least not through wax and water. It's probably best to let the candles and water rest, and to attempt a different method—perhaps one mentioned elsewhere in this book.

Molten Wax Divination

This method is time-consuming, but as stated before is often found to be more effective.

You need a double-boiler for this. If you don't have one, a coffee can placed in a large pot of water will do. Not glamorous, true, but it works.

In the top of the double-boiler (or coffee can, with label removed) place about one cup of crumbled solid wax. Sheets of wax are available at hobby and craft stores, and the paraffin wax used for canning (available at most grocery stores) is fine. Beeswax is best, but again is quite expensive.

The wax should be plain white. Coloring it not only adds to the expense, but also to the work involved.

Fill the bottom pot about one-third with water and place the top or can into it. Heat the water until boiling. The wax should begin melting almost immediately. Next to the stove place a box of baking soda, just in case the wax catches fire. There is little danger of this when using a double-boiler, but be prepared just in case.

While the wax is melting, fill a vessel with water as directed in the first method. When the wax is melted, remove the can or double-boiler carefully from the pot with holders, and take it to the vessel of water. While concentrating on your question (or clearing your mind) quickly pour half of the wax into the water. Place the can or pot back in the double-boiler and turn off the heat. Now return to the table and look at the wax image you've just created.

If it hasn't solidified yet, wait. Then, gingerly dunk it completely under water, to firm all the wax, and finally remove it.

The impact of the molten wax hitting the water and then suddenly hardening will have created a solid three-dimensional object. Sometimes it is little more than abstract, at other times it is sharply definite.

Look at the piece for a while, turning it over in your hands, searching for its identity. Once you have recognized a shape, interpret it (see chapter 3: Techniques).

As with any occult art, especially divination, you will improve with practice.

You left half of the wax in the double-boiler, right? Pour it into the water to make another shape. The two can be read together if the same question—or lack of such—was asked each time, and this will enrich your field of symbols.

15

MIRROR MAGIC

Mirror, mirror, on the wall,
Who's the fairest of them all?

The sorceress queen's plea to her magic mirror in the old fairy tale we now know as *Snow White* is an echo of practices as ancient as time itself. Like many of the tools of magic, the mirror is a device patterned after nature.

The first mirrors were lakes. On a still day when the water lies flat a fairly good reflection can be seen. In attempts to capture this phenomenon stones were polished, metal was buffed, and finally glass was produced that when backed with a thin layer of silver, produced a perfect reflecting surface—an absolutely clear lake "frozen" to be used at will.

Mirrors (and all reflecting surfaces) have long captured our imaginations. Folklore is full of references to mirrors and so is magic, though such practices are nearly forgotten today.

The symbolism of the mirror is simple and yet complex. It is held to be sacred to the moon, for as the moon reflects the sun's light, so is the mirror an object of reflection. Since it is a lunar symbol, the mirrors used in magic are generally round.

Also, mirrors allow us to see things we could not see without their aid—not only the physical but higher things, such as memories of past lives, glimpses of the future, or visions of events occurring at the same moment in another place.

Mirror magic was probably at its heyday during the classical Greece and Rome periods. Polished mirrors of bronze were used in magical as well as cosmetic rituals. Most of these mirrors were small and held in the hand.

One old technique of inducing clairvoyance is to catch the light of a fire in the shiny blade of a sword or knife; the reflection, thus caught and concentrated upon, causes visions. This is simply another form of metallic mirror magic.

Though practices such as this are still used, most mirror magic today is performed with glass mirrors. Older mirrors are not necessarily better, since they tend to have imperfections (such as the silvering peeling off or "bunching"), which may interfere with most workings.

For quick rituals, you can even utilize a pocket compact mirror, though this is much easier for women. More than one spell has been cast while a woman pretended to check her makeup.

Always remember that the mirror is simply a tool, a link with the moon, with your subconscious, and ultimately, with nature herself.

The following details the preparation of a magic mirror. Though the magic mirror cannot be used for all the spells in this chapter, its preparation is recommended, for once finished, it will be ready for use at any time. Magic is often spontaneous, and you should be prepared for practically anything.

The Magic Mirror

Find a round mirror of thirteen to thirty inches in diameter.

Ideally, it should be encased in a similarly round frame, painted black, but make do with what you have.

After purchasing the mirror, take it home and wash its face carefully with clean water. If you wish, next wash it with an infusion of mugwort—one teaspoon to one cup of water. Cool before use.

When the mirror has dried, cover its face with a black cloth and lay it where it won't be touched until the full moon. On that night, expose the mirror to its rays, preferably outside but through a window if necessary. Charge the magic mirror in the moonlight, and say the following or similar words:

Lady of the moon,
you who sees all things and knows all knowledge,
I consecrate this mirror with your glowing rays
that it may illuminate my works of magic and my life.

Now take it inside and hang it on the eastern wall in your bedroom, or the room in which you practice magic. Keep the mirror covered when not in use.

Expose the mirror to the moon at least three times a year. When it gets dusty (if it should), wash with a mugwort infusion or plain water. Never use an ammonia-based spray to clean your mirror, for ammonia destroys all magic!

If you wish, you may use a "psychic"-type oil (such as clove or nutmeg) to trace a crescent on its back, thus marking it with the moon's sign.

Never use the mirror for anything other then magic. Keep a separate mirror for everyday uses.

Following are several spells, most of which can be done with a magic mirror.

CHANT FOR SCRYING

Stand before a magic mirror, remove its covering, and chant the following until visions appear:

> Mirror of moonlight,
> mirror of glass,
> allow me to see
> what e'er shall pass.
> Sweep clear the veil
> that lies before me.
> This is my will,
> so mote it be!

The best time to scry in your magic mirror is dawn, dusk, or at night.

FAR MEMORY

Set a white candle aflame in a darkened room and place in a position so that it illuminates your face as you stand before the mirror, but itself isn't reflected.

Say the following:

Oracle of lunar light,
send me now the second sight.

Gaze into your reflection's eyes, or just above and between them. Gradually, your reflection will dissolve and you will see another face appear; it will be that of a former life. It should be unmistakeably familiar to you.

With practice this can be used to learn a great deal about past lives. Try to "tune in" on the face. Attempt to see the rest of the body, clothing, jewelry, backgrounds—anything that would help you place the period and location.

Just seeing the face may trigger unexpected emotional reactions within you; note these and you may begin to remember people and events that have been locked away inside your far memory.

Sometimes this works better in near darkness; adjust the amount of light that hits your face until you have achieved desired results.

A SIMPLE MIRROR SPELL

Stand before your magic mirror. Set twin candles of the appropriate colors (see appendix I) on either side. With a grease pencil (or, as my first teacher always used, a bright red lipstick) or water-soluble paint, draw a rune or symbol of your need. As you draw it, be sure to do so in the space your face occupies in the reflection. See the symbol becoming infused with your reflection, and know that your need will be satisfied in your life.

Close your eyes and firmly visualize your need, then leave the area. This rune should be allowed to remain on the mirror until morning, when it should be wiped away using a cloth, preferably without looking at it.

A DIVINATION

Take a small round mirror and dip it into water (preferably a lake or stream, but a full sink or bathtub will do). Remove it immediately and catch your reflection. If it is disfigured, beware! Evil may be working against you or you may soon face problems. Perform protective magic.

If the reflection is clear, however, no problems are foreseeable.

ANOTHER DIVINATION

If you wish to discover the conditions of a person far from you—if they be well or sick, in trouble or safe—do this:

Stand before the mirror in near darkness. Visualize the person's face as you last saw her or him; make this as complete a picture as possible. Now hold the visualization of the face and wait for any changes to occur—a scar forming on the face may indicate physical difficulties; a smile may suggest happiness, and so on.

The whole image may be blotted out with a symbol, and this should then be interpreted to determine your friend's condition.

With practice this can be a great aid to establishing links with, or at least "checking up" on friends far away.

A MIRROR PORTAL

When you feel that evil is within your house, obtain a small, round mirror. Paint the back black and devise some means of hanging it high in a corner next to the ceiling of the room in which the evil feels strongest.

If possible, hang the mirror so that it is at a 45-degree angle to the wall.

This mirror shall act as a "portal" through which all evil in the house shall pass into outer space where it will be dispersed and destroyed.

Once you hang up the mirror, stand in the room and see the evil swirling around you in a counterclockwise motion, thick and black like a foul fog. Then, look up to the mirror and visualize a great door opening there, a door into the vacuum of space. See the black, evil-infested fog being sucked through the mirror, away from your home, and out of your life.

If you have trouble doing this, repeat until you feel the room is free of negativity. Once this is achieved (it may feel like the room gives a sigh afterward), stand on something to enable you to reach the mirror, and with the forefinger of your power hand, trace an equal-armed cross over the face of the mirror to "lock" it, so that it becomes a one-way portal. Evil can go out, but it can't come back in.

Make this cross by moving your forefinger from the top of the mirror, down across its face to the bottom in a straight line, then lifting the finger and placing it at the left side and tracing a line straight across to the middle of the right side.

Leave the mirror in its position for at least seven days. After this, remove it and cleanse with a strong vinegar or ammonia solution to rid it of all negative vibrations. Do not perform this spell with your magic mirror.

SCRYING BY MOON AND MIRROR

With a small, round, and convex mirror large enough to hold in your hand (car rearview mirrors are ideal) go out on a cool, clear night when the full moon rides at her peak in the sky.

Sit comfortably and catch the moon's reflections in the mirror. Concentrate on the tiny pinpoint of silvery-white light, and begin to slowly move the mirror, fractions of inches to all sides, watching the moon's image gyrate and wiggle on the surface of the mirror.

This will induce a psychic state after several minutes, so long as you do this alone and are not disturbed.

TO IMPROVE THE APPEARANCE

Stand before the magic mirror, alone and naked. If possible, every part of your body that needs improvement should be visible. This will require a large mirror, at least thirty inches in diameter.

Gaze at your reflection in subdued candlelight. Study it, and inspect it. As you do so say:

Clear as crystal,
clear as air.
Make my form be
fine and fair.

Then, with your powers of visualization, begin forming a new body. Smooth out wrinkles. Flatten bulges. Increase muscles. Perform all changes you would see on your body with your mind.

Hold this for as long as you can, up to thirteen minutes or so. Afterward, look at your body again and say the following words once more:

Clear as crystal,
clear as air,
make my form be
fine and fair.

Repeat this spell every morning and evening and back it up with exercise, dieting, and whatever else will aid you in achieving your goal.

THE SEND-BACK SPELL

If you feel that evil is being directed toward you, from known or unknown persons or entities, this spell can be utilized. Even if you don't know for sure that someone is trying to hurt you, perform this spell anyway, just in case.

Set up a small, round mirror (not your magic mirror) so that it is leaning against a wall, or set it in a holder so that the mirror is parallel with the wall. Before it place a black candle in a plain holder. Be sure the candle is reflected in the mirror.

Now, get a large white candle and place it away from the mirror (preferably where it won't be reflected) and light it. This is done to ensure that the black candle doesn't attract any evil forces.

Now, standing before the mirror and black candle, strike a match and as you light the candle, begin chanting:

Black, black
send evil back.

Repeat this chant while looking at the candle for a few moments and then leave the room.

After an hour snuff the candle's flame (without using your fingers—use a candle snuffer or the blade of a knife) and put it and the mirror away. Then quench the white candle's flame and place it safely out of sight. Repeat the spell for seven nights or until you feel the evil is gone.

This spell sends any evil forces which may be directed toward you back to the original senders. It is a defensive measure only.

THE COIN AND CAULDRON SPELL

This is a vestige of the metal mirror magic performed by our ancestors. The "mirror" here is a large, silver coin. (If American, it should have been minted prior to 1964, when silver in coins was largely replaced with other metals. I use a 1961 Liberty Bell half dollar in my magic. Since silver is symbolic of the moon, there is a definite reason for this insistence on genuine silver coins.)

On the night of the full moon, fill a cauldron (or any bowl painted black inside and out) with water. Take it and the coin outside in a place where you will not be disturbed.

Set the cauldron or bowl on the ground. Holding the coin up to the moon, say:

Lady of light,
lady of night,
strengthen the sight
in this my rite.

Place the coin into the water. When it rests on the bottom, adjust the cauldron and coin so that it captures and reflects the moon's light. It will appear to be a round, shining silvery-white object on the blackness of the cauldron's interior.

Sitting or kneeling comfortably, gaze at the coin with half-opened eyes. The second sight will come.

The Broken Mirror

Break a mirror and you'll have seven years of bad luck, right?

That's what the superstition says.

Actually, while there are several explanations for this piece of misinformation, one of the most sensible (in magical thought) is that you'll have to buy another mirror! In the fourteenth century, the first modern, breakable mirrors were produced in Venice. These were quite costly. One can imagine the future of a servant who accidentally broke a mirror. He or she would indeed have bad luck from the master or mistress!

If your magic mirror breaks, or any other, don't worry. It is still valuable in magic. Carefully collect all the large fragments and place them in a clear glass jar. Sweep up the mirror dust and pour this into the jar too, then cork or cap tightly and set in a sunny window of the home.

This will automatically keep evil or negative influences from entering your dwelling, for the thousand tiny splinters each act as a protective mirror.

Keep the bottle well dusted and it shall serve you well. If you wish, glue a small, round mirror on top of the bottle.

When finished buy another mirror and prepare it to ensure you have one when needed.

16

RAIN, FOG,
AND STORM MAGIC

The weather has long been a subject of fear, joy, anger, and frustration. For those who aren't in touch with nature, an unexpected rainstorm may ruin a picnic, or a bolt of lightning may strike a home and burn its contents.

Magicians and Witches through the centuries have known methods of working with the weather and also how to control it to a certain extent.

Here is the magic of lightning, thick banks of fog, gentle rains, and slamming storms. Though there are countless spells to bring rain, only a few are included here, for too often the effects come as desired—and then can't be stopped.

Rain

Rain is the cleansing, purifying cycle of nature. As such, a rainstorm is an excellent time to perform spells of this type, such as the following:

TO BREAK A BAD HABIT

With water colors or chalk, draw or write the bad habit on a piece of paper. Immediately take it out into the rain. Let the rain dissolve and disperse the water colors or chalk. So shall your habit dissolve, cleansed by the sanctifying rain.

A RAIN DIVINATION

When rain is falling lightly outside, do the following: on a flat surface such as a pie pan or cookie sheet, sprinkle an even layer of powdered spice, such as cinnamon. When the surface is completely covered to an even depth, take it outside, and stand in the rain. Ask your question and then run back inside. The raindrops will have disturbed the spice to etch patterns or symbols into it. Sit quietly and gaze at the spice until you have perceived the answer.

Fog Magic

Fog magic is best performed on a night when the mists curl tightly around you. There should be almost no light in the vicinity for the spells and magic to be most effective; you must be alone with the fog.

If there is a light, move so that it is behind you. It will light the fog before you, but you won't be disturbed by its glow.

Fog obliterates the outside world; within it you are alone, terribly alone, with only the ground you stand upon bonding you to the earth. Fog magic is unstructured, as changing as the substance itself. Here are some guidelines.

CHARGING THE FOG

Take the expanse of fog before you. Charge it with a specific emotional value: hatred, joy, love, frustration, fear, peace, terror—experiment to see if you can do it.

See these emotions leaving your body as glowing rays of energy. See it stabbing into the fog, lighting it up, until it is positively glowing.

Now, shrug off the feeling. Step into that fog and feel the effects this has on you. Those emotions should be flooding through you.

If you are successful, take the exercise one step further. Charge the fog bank in front of you with waves of radiating heat. Walk into it and you should feel warmer.

When this technique has been mastered, it can be used for practical purposes the next time you find yourself out walking in fog. If you feel terror, charge the fog before you with peace or courage. Continue doing this as you walk along; within moments your fear will have vanished.

Or perhaps your finances aren't what they should be. Charge the fog directly before you with golden energy; see it glittering with gold coins, floating crazily in the mist-shrouded air. As you walk, "scoop up" these coins and deposit them in your pocket.

This can be used for many purposes.

PROTECTIVE FOG

Again, when you find yourself walking through thick fog, visualize it swirling around your body counterclockwise, forming a tight cocoon of brilliantly shining white light.

Once mastered, this will be an excellent protection against the unknown that may lie in waiting in the mists.

A MAGICAL FOG EXERCISE

To develop your powers of concentration, and also as an excellent demonstration of power, stand in the fog in a place where you can see it (during the day, or near a light).

Stare directly ahead of you into the fog while relaxing. Your goal is to burn holes clear through the fog. Don't attempt to force the fog to evaporate; simply stare steadily into the fog. If you are working properly, the holes will appear and continue on for infinity.

A FOG VISUALIZATION

When you feel your mind being invaded, or when you sense that someone is trying to read your thoughts, visualize a thick, impenetrable fog swirling counterclockwise within your head. See its dark, constantly moving mass. This will effectively stop any psychic eavesdropping as long as the visualization is maintained.

While there may be little need of using them, there are people who, knowingly or not, try to get inside our heads. This visualization will block their attempts.

Storms

Electrical storms are times of great energy. The electrical energy of lightning mixes with the magnetic forces of water (rain), thus creating an extremely powerful magical brew.

Any spells cast during a violent storm will be supercharged. For this reason, such times—especially when they occur after dark—usually set any good magician or Witch working quickly.

First, the house itself must be protected, as well as its contents and those residing within its walls.

SPELL FOR THE HOME DURING A LIGHTNING STORM

Light one white and one yellow candle and put them in a place of importance in the home (a magical or religious altar is ideal).

Walk through the house, room by room, chanting these words until you have visited every room, closet, cupboard, and entrance at least once:

> Mistress of the gentle rain,
> master of the storm,
> guard against the ill and bane,
> shield me from harm.
> And while fire flies through the air
> and raindrops fiercely blast,
> keep my loved ones in your care
> 'til the storm has passed.
> > Wind, wind, guard my kin.
> > Flame, flame, do not maim.
> > Rain, rain, quickly wane.
> > Earth, earth, guard my worth.

The house is then sealed and safe-guarded until the storm is clear of the area.

LIGHTNING MAGIC

Now, down to business. All amulets, talismans, lucky charms, and personal power objects can be charged with the glancing energies that rain down from the sky.

Take the objects to be charged (only objects that you feel require the electrical energy of lightning, such as those concerned with healing, protection, and so on) outside and place them in an area where they will be free from the possibility of washing away, but still fully exposed to the rain and lightning.

Do not place them upon the roof of a house or other structure. You might wish to tie them to a tree, or place them in a large container. Do whatever is necessary to ensure their safety during the charging process.

When the storm has passed, bring them inside, dry carefully, and put in a safe place. They are highly charged and should be vibrating with energy.

PROTECTION AGAINST LIGHTNING

If the lightning is fierce outside, you may wish to make an anti-lightning charm for your house to protect it from straying strikes. To make this charm, take about a teaspoon each of parsley, elderberries, mistletoe; add an acorn and a bit of crumbled fern. Place these in a small bag made of a white material, fill it up with coarse rock salt, and hang it as high as you can in the house. An attic is an excellent place. This will safeguard your home from lightning.

Traditionally, an oak tree is planted near the home to protect it from lightning, so if you live in an area subject to many intense storms, you may consider this.

And, finally, one last lightning charm. If you discover after the storm has passed a tree that has been hit by lightning, try to procure a small piece of the charred, blackened wood. Bury something for the tree if you do take some of the wood. It has been said that if a sick person holds the lightning-struck wood, rubs it on the afflicted part of the body, and then throws it behind his or her back, it will remove any disease.

When the Storm Is Over

When rain and lightning have stopped, but you're not sure if the storm is completely passed, look to the sky if it is daylight. If you see birds, it is an excellent sign. For certainty, however, watch the birds in flight, then chant aloud as you do:

Birds of the air,
fly without care.
Will it rain here?
Will it rain there?

When they fly off, stop chanting and look closely in the direction in which they leave; if it is the east, the storm is passed. If they fly south, a fiercer storm may be headed your way. When the birds fly to the west, the rain will continue soon, but if they go north, it will be clear for the rest of the day. Or, in rhyming form:

To the east, 'twill be clear,
To the south, storm you'll hear,
To the west, never end,
To the north, sun descend.

To Affect the Weather

As stated before, it can be dangerous to control the weather. At certain times, however, such spells are necessary. If they are used in earnest and genuine need, no problems should arise from their use.

Remember that Mother Nature is a powerful force. It is not easy persuading her to change her (weather) mind.

FOR RAIN

Burn together out-of-doors in a wild, lone place heather, fern, and broom. As the smoke rises up, visualize it forming into clouds, and these clouds turning black, and finally belching forth their store of rain to the ground.

A RAIN BREW

Fill a bucket, pot, or cauldron with water. Add a few dried, crumbled fern leaves and take it, with a brand-new broom, outside where you wish the rain to fall. With the sweeping end of the broom, stir the cauldron in a clockwise direction, gently increasing the speed until you are thrashing the water wildly and the broom's handle seems almost to spin of its own volition.

As you are doing this, visualize a rain storm in all its wild splendor—the rain landing with thuds on the dry, cracked ground, sending up clouds of dust; the wind whipping the trees and your own clothing; the smell of thunder—the awesome power of nature pouring forth all her wrath into a tremendous outburst.

When you can vividly imagine the rain slamming down on you and the wind thrashing, lift the broom's wetted end up to the sky and shake it with all your might. Dip it back into the cauldron and repeat the process, still visualizing the storm playing out all its forces around you.

Throw the broom down. Lift the container and hurl its contents upward.

Be prepared!

TO HALT AN APPROACHING STORM

Seek out an axe that has been used for chopping wood. Snatch it up, run to the boundary of your property, and raise the axe above your head. Swing it around (counterclockwise) in the very face of the rushing current, as if chopping at it. The wind will die down, the storm will move somewhere else, sparing you and your property. The magic of the sharp-edged axe has done its work.

At one time this was popular with farmers for whom a rain would have destroyed an impending harvest.

TO STOP RAIN

Make a cross with two sticks (an equal-armed cross), sprinkle salt on top of this, and the rain should cease. Do this outside.

Naturally, these techniques might work, and then again, might not. They have been formulated during the last several thousand years out of our desire to be in control of our environment. This cannot happen. We cannot control the weather any more than we can control earthquakes. Nature must be allowed her release or even greater trouble will surely follow.

Let the earth have her way; let her blow off steam periodically, and only in times of desperate need use these last spells.

This is the one condition under which they will work.

In closing this chapter, here's a practical note. It is said that boiling eggs under the open sky will cause rain to fall. The next time you're out camping bring them preboiled, unless you want a soggy vacation!

17

SEA MAGIC

Sea magic is that which is practiced near the ocean, or with the objects that the ocean fashions or transforms.

The sea has for millennia been worshipped, feared, consecrated, prayed to, sacrificed to, and otherwise revered. It has been the abode of goddesses and gods, mermaids and mermen, undines and serpents—hideous monsters and fetching sirens who lured sailors to their deaths on treacherous rocks.

Beneath its waves lie ancient, fabled lands and civilizations—Atlantis, Lemuria, Lyonesse, to name a few—and from it all life emerged. Thus, the sea is both the beginning and the end, alpha and omega—the source of all life and that which nourishes it. In ancient times, as today, population centers were located close to rivers or on the coastline. Here was easy access to food—fish, shellfish, and seaweeds—as well as a platform on which crafts of reeds and pitch, timber and hemp rope, and later of more sophisticated boat design could float and travel to distant lands.

Those people who depended on the sea for their food and, thus their very lives, personified it; gods and goddesses arose from its depths and spread their arms lovingly to embrace the simple peoples, or blew up waves that crushed their fragile boats and washed villages away.

Just as streams, wells, and rivers have been revered, so too has the sea: along with religious rites, magic was performed, as it still is today.

Many of the old deities of the sea are now the stuff of books—Poseidon, Isis, Llyr, Pontus, Mari, Neptune, Shony, Tiamat, Dylan, Manannan—all and many more have had libations poured to them, incense offered to them, sacrifices given to them.

What the books don't seem to know is that they live still; their whispers are heard in the ocean's sighs and their powers wax and wane with the moon. They lie waiting to rise up and be recognized again.

Though you don't have to worship the sea or its deities to practice sea magic, you must respect it as a vast storehouse of power. It is our ancestral mother, older than the continents upon which we live, older than mountain or tree or stone. It is time itself.

Though sea magic is best performed near the ocean, many of the following spells can be altered slightly and performed anywhere, so long as you can acquire some of the tools.

A bowl full of water into which you've poured salt will work in a pinch for the ocean, as will a tub of salted water. Search in antique shops and specialty houses for shells, sand, seaweed, and so on.

Sea magic is as mysterious and flexible as the oceans themselves. Here is some of its magic.

The Tides

The tides are an essential aspect of sea magic, as the moon is to all magic. They mark the heartbeat of the ocean; the fluxes of power that can be tapped and drawn upon in magic.

There are four phases of the tides and the moon, which is the tide's ruler:

1. Flow, when the tide is coming in (from low to high tide)

2. High tide, the highest the ocean rises on the beach in any twelve-hour period

3. Ebb, when the tide is receding (from high to low tide)

4. Low tide, the lowest the ocean falls on the beach in any twelve-hour period

Low tide is generally not used in magic. It is a good time for meditation and introspection, however, and also for looking into past lives.

All positive, productive spells should be performed during the tide's flow. This includes fertility, money, love, healing, and so on.

High tide is traditionally the best time of all to do spells of any sort—positive or negative, good or bane.

When the sea is ebbing, spells of a destructive or banishing nature are best performed.

There are two high and two low tides every day. Most sport-fishing stores and libraries have tide tables, as do newspapers in coastal towns and cities. Chart the tides the day you wish to do a spell, if you live near the ocean, and perform it as close to the proper "phase" as you can for maximum results. This can be taken into account for every spell or magical working you perform, but isn't necessary.

For an important ritual, the highest tide of the month is a most auspicious time. You can determine this by studying a tidal table for a month and finding the largest number of feet the ocean rises on the beach. This is the highest tide, and it always corresponds with the full moon. If you can't wait, don't worry—it won't harm the spell.

In addition to the extra powers at large in the sea on the high tide, there is also a practical reason for charting the tides. Rites performed on a secluded stretch of beach are truly evocative, magical experiences, but if the tide is flowing and the area is rocky and faced with sheer cliffs, you could find yourself trapped with nowhere to go.

This almost happened to me one night. After a magical night on the beach, the tide rose dangerously high. I had to climb over a series of jagged cliffs in near darkness to return to my car. Glancing back, I saw the beach underwater. After that I always charted the tides!

The Tools

The tools of sea magic are found in the ocean or tossed up by the waves on the beach. They are natural and man-made; ancient as the sea itself and as new and fresh as the dawn. Though the tools vary from place to place and era to era, here are some of the best known.

Sea Shells

Gifts of the sea, shells are used to represent the oceanic deities. Long, spiralled shells signify the gods, while round shells symbolize the goddesses. Cowries have been used for centuries for the latter purpose.

Many sea Witches and magicians place shells on their altars for this very reason when performing sea magic at home.

When spells are done by the seashore, a protective circle can be marked out with a ring of shells gathered for that specific purpose.

Shells are strung and worn to promote fertility, or to attract money, since they were once used as money.

Take a large univalve (one-piece) shell and hold it close to your ear. You will hear the voice of the sea. Let it speak to you. You may hear messages of the future or past; or the sound of the sea may still your mind so psychic messages may be received.

A special shell you find on the beach may be fashioned into a protective or lucky amulet.

A shell in the home can be an indicator of the sea. Hold it to your ear: if the sounds within it are loud, the sea is rough; if soft, the sea is smooth and calm.

A shell placed at the entrance of the house ensures that luck will enter it.

Conches or other very large univalves are blown at seaside rites to dispel negativity and to invite the gods and good spirits to be present at rituals and spells.

Driftwood

Driftwood, infused with salt by the sea, dried by the sun on the beach, is the natural fuel for mystic bonfires, which often play a part in magic (see chapter 7: Fire Magic).

Driftwood can be used in spells. Take an appropriate piece, and carve your need on it with a knife. Throw the driftwood into the sea, imploring it to grant your need.

A smaller piece of driftwood can be adorned with protective symbols and worn as an amulet or talisman to attract or repel forces, depending on your desires.

A sort of magic wand can be made from a piece of driftwood; with this wand circles can be drawn on the sand in which magic can be performed. It can also be used to sketch runes into the sand. There are no rules for the size, shape, or type of wood used; whatever the sea has to offer is fine.

Fishing Floats

On the beaches of the Pacific Ocean in the northwestern part of the United States, fishing floats are cast up on the beach. This is also true of coastlines in many parts of the world.

Many years ago all such floats, which are used to hold up fishing nets, were manufactured of glass, usually of a blue or green tint. The glass is thick and the floats "pop" when dropped or broken, and on the base of the ball is a slightly raised mass of glass, where the ball was sealed tightly during its manufacture.

Unfortunately, most fishing floats used today are plastic. If you do find a glass ball on the beach you are extremely fortunate. If not, buy one in an antique or gift shop. Be sure the ball was actually used in the sea, as this charges and empowers it.

Whether or not you find an old or new ball, take it to the sea at high tide. Dip it thrice into the water and say the following:

Orb of blue (or green) glass here I charge thee
to be a psychic boon to me.
When touched with salt your power's free!
This is my will, so mote it be.

Take the ball home, wrap in blue-green cloth, and store in a safe place.

The fishing float may now be used as a crystal ball for scrying. Take it out, anoint its base with a dab of salt water, hold it in the cloth, and scry.

Holed Stones

If you find a stone with a hole pierced through it on the seashore, take it, for it is a valuable magical tool. The holed or "holey" stone is hung up in the home for protection, worn on a cord around the neck for the same purposes, and is used for many other magical purposes.

Take a holed stone, find a stick that fits tightly through the hole, and lodge it firmly inside. Throw it into the sea. Love will come to you.

To see the spirits of the sea, take the holed stone with you to the ocean at night, at high tide. Close one eye, facing the sea, and put the holed stone to the other. Look through the hole and you may see spirits.

For healing place a holed stone into your bath water. Add salt and step in. The stone should be used for this purpose only.

The holed stone is one of the most valuable tools of magic, and it is free, a gift from the sea. Since it is a symbol of eternity and the female force of nature, it is not only a good luck piece, and an effective magical tool, it is indeed sacred.

Seaweed

While seaweed is an important food source in many parts of the world, here in the West it is rarely used, except in processing and preserving different foods and products such as toothpaste and ice cream. There are many magical uses of seaweed, however.

Dry a small piece of any type outdoors. When it is fully dry, hang it in the home and it will keep the structure safe from fire.

Dried seaweed is also used for kindling the fires on the beach, and is hung outside as a weather indicator. When the seaweed is shriveled up, the weather will be sunny. When it swells and feels damp to the touch, however, chances are wet weather is to be expected.

A small piece of seaweed placed in a jar of whiskey, tightly capped and set in a sunny window, may attract money to your household. The bottle should be shaken every day.

The following is a collection of sea spells as they are performed today. They can be done by anyone, provided you are close to the sea, or even a large lake or river.

A CLEANSING

When you feel cursed, hexed, angry, or cluttered up with fears and anxieties, walk into the sea at dawn. Let the waves splash over you, and say something like the following:

> I perform this act of cleansing
> in the place of the beginning of all life.
> Waves lap body and spirit,
> dust falls into the cleansing sea.
> I am renewed and fresh.
> Fresh as the sea.

Now walk from the water onto the sand and let the winds dry your body. It is done.

TO FALL INTO A TRANCE

Sit and close your eyes on the beach, above the high tide line. Relax and listen to the crashings and flowings of the ocean, and you will entrance yourself.

Or, watch the reflections of a full moon on the ocean; follow its path with your eyes to the horizon and then back again toward you, repeating this until you fall into a trance.

A SEA WITCHES BOTTLE

Take a large jar with a tight-fitting lid (such as a canning or mayonnaise jar) and a bag to the ocean very early in the morning, preferably just after a high tide.

Walk on the beach gathering small pieces of driftwood, shells, rocks; those natural objects that have been thrown up onto the sand by the waves. Place these in a bag.

When you have gathered several things, stop, sit on the beach, and spread them out before you. Place each in the jar singly, saying as you do:

Amulet of the sea that I have found,
protective energy in you is bound.

When each piece is placed in the jar, add a half-handful of fresh sand and then fill with seawater.

Tightly cap or cork the jar and take it home. On your property, near the front porch if possible, dig a hole in the ground large enough to contain the bottle. As you place it in the hole, say the following:

Waves on sand, the tides in motion,
you are now a silent ocean.
Avert all evil to the sea,
this is my will, so mote it be.

Cover the bottle and return the earth to a normal appearance. If you cannot bury the bottle, secret it in a flowerpot, cover with dirt or sand, and place it somewhere outside, near the home.

The jar will act as a protective device for your home and all who reside within it.

TO SEND FORTH POWER

Sit on the beach and meditate. Visualize your need. Feel the power. When the energy is at its peak, hold it until a wave crashes on the sand and then release it. The wave will magnify the power tremendously.

A SEA LOVE SPELL

On a Friday at high tide, preferably at night, take an apple and some cloves to the ocean. On the beach, stud the apple with the cloves, marking out the rune of love in it thrice (see appendix II).

Now hold the apple in your power hand and infuse it with your desire for love, saying such words as this:

Apple of love, cloves of fire,
this is my need, my desire!

Throw the apple as far away from you out to sea as you are able. So shall it be.

THE BUCKET SPELL

Fill an iron-bound bucket in the sea and throw the water back. Repeat this twice more, and each time as you return the water to the sea say:

I return to you what is yours,
return to me what is mine.

This spell is used to bring sailors and fishermen home safely from the sea.

TO COMMUNICATE WITH ONE AT SEA

Fill a large crystal vessel with seawater. Place this on the sand and, sitting before it, hold your hands palms down over the water's surface and vividly visualize the face of the person you wish to contact. Remove your hands and with your imagination "write" your message upon the surface of the water.

Next, throw the water into the ocean. This spell will carry your message to one at sea.

A SEA SPELL

This is an all-purpose spell.

Go to the seashore when the tide has begun to rise (after low tide but before high). Upon the sand just above the line where the waves are breaking, draw a circle about one foot in diameter with your fingers.

Next, draw a rune or image of your need within the circle you've formed. As you draw it, visualize blue liquid flame striking the sand where your finger digs into it. When the figure is complete, see the power resting within the furrows on the wet sand like phosphorescent water in a perfect pattern of your need. Firmly visualize.

Now, step back and wait for the waves to rise and wash away your design, releasing the energy to go forth and do your bidding.

One day, while performing this spell on the beach during a light rain, I stood waiting for the wave to wash it away. As it did, I felt a bolt of energy shoot up from the rune I'd sketched on the sand and hit me in the chest. It was an actual physical sensation. The energy went forth and did indeed bring into manifestation my need.

A SHELL SPELL

Gather a sufficient quantity of shells upon the beach. They don't have to be perfect, polished specimens, but should be fairly whole and complete. Do this, of course, at the proper tide.

At a secluded stretch of beach stand holding the shells in your hand (or a bag) and watch the waves for a while. Every seventh or ninth wave should be larger than the others. While this is supposed to be only superstition, I have observed the waves on the West Coast of the United States occurring in this series.

Just after the larger wave, lay the shells onto the freshly washed sand in a crude image of your need. Or, if you wish, simply mark out with shells the letters spelling your desire.

Work quickly, then stand back and wait for the high wave to return. If, when it does, your shells are tumbled back with it into the sea, your desire shall be granted.

AFTERWORD

Dawn. Far above the misted forest, a wild bird heralds the sun's reappearance with a cry of ecstasy. Through the moss-covered trees a man walks, his feet crunching softly on the forest floor.

Peering through the shrouded air, he sees a tree, smiles, and walks to stand beneath its gnarled branches.

After pulling a charred stick from his coat pocket, the man draws a round symbol on a leaf while his breath frosts the air. Using a fallen branch, he ties the leaf to the tree's broad trunk, then steps back to admire his work.

Sunlight spills into the wood, burning away the mist with shining rays.

Seeing this, the man dusts off his hands, gives one last look at the tree, and moves to return home.

A breeze shakes the wood. Light pours suddenly onto the old tree's trunk. Wind swirls tightly around it, tugging at the branch until it breaks free. The breeze catches the inscribed leaf and, gleaming golden brown in the light, it swirls higher and higher, past the crying bird and on to the sun.

Magic has begun.

Appendix I

COLORS

WHITE: protection, peace, purity, truth

GREEN: healing, money, prosperity, luck, fertility

BROWN: physical objects, healing for animals, houses and homes

PINK: emotional love, friendships

RED: sexual love, passion, energy, enthusiasm, courage

YELLOW: clairvoyance, divination, studying, learning, the mind

PURPLE: power, healing deadly diseases

BLUE: healing, meditation, tranquility

ORANGE: strength, authority, attraction, luck

BLACK: absorption of negativity, destruction of negativity

Appendix II

RUNES

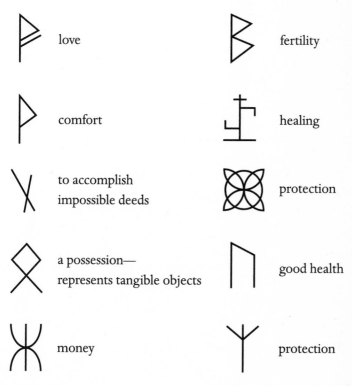

love

fertility

comfort

healing

to accomplish
impossible deeds

protection

a possession—
represents tangible objects

good health

money

protection

Appendix III

HERBS

Recommended herbs for various magical needs are listed alphabetically below the proper heading:

Business
Benzoin
Cinnamon

Divination

Anise
Ash
Bay Laurel
Bistort
Chicory
Cinnamon
Cinquefoil
Eyebright

Goldenrod
Gum Mastic
Juniper
Marigold
Mugwort
Nutmeg
Patchouli
Rose

Rosemary
Sandalwood
Star Anise
Thyme
Wormwood
Yarrow

Fertility

Cucumber
Mandrake
Myrtle
Oak

Pine
Pomegranate
Poppy
Rose

Sunflower
Walnut

Healing

Amaranth
Anemone
Apple
Ash
Balm of Gilead
Carnation
Cinnamon
Eucalyptus

Hops
Lavender
Myrrh
Narcissus
Onion
Peppermint
Red Geranium
Rose

Rosemary
Rue
Sage
Sandalwood
Spearmint
Thistle
Violet

Love

Apple
Aster
Caraway
Coriander
Cumin
Jasmine

Lavender
Lovage
Marjoram
Meadowsweet
Myrtle
Orange

Orris
Rosemary
Tormentil
Vervain
Violet
Yarrow

Mental Powers

Balm of Gilead
Caraway
Clove

Hazel
Honeysuckle
Lavender

Periwinkle
Rosemary
Rue

Money

Almond
Basil
Bergamot
Bryony
Camomile
Cinquefoil
Cloves
High John the
  Conqueror
Honeysuckle
Hyssop
Jasmine
Mint
Patchouli
Pine
Sage
Sassafras
Vervain
Wheat

Peace

Basil
Cumin
Frankincense
Rose
Valerian

Protection

Angelica
Ash
Balm of Gilead
Bay Laurel
Cyclamen
Dill
Fennel
Fern
Hyssop
Mistletoe
Mullein
Peony
Rose Geranium
Rosemary
Rowan
Rue
St. John's Wort
Snapdragon
Tarragon
Vervain

Purification

Anise
Basil
Bay Laurel
Dragon's Blood
Elder
Frankincense
Hyssop
Lavender
Lemon
Lemon Verbena
Lovage
Myrrh
Orange
Peppermint
Pine
Rosemary
Rue
Saffron
Sandalwood
Solomon's Seal

Youth

Cowslip	Linden	Rosemary
Lavender	Oak	Sage

BIBLIOGRAPHY

Powers of the Earth

Bord, Janet and Colin. *Mysterious Britain*. New York: Doubleday, 1972.

———. *The Secret Country*. New York: Warner, 1976.

Hitching, Francis. *Earth Magic*. New York: Pocket Books, 1978.

Michell, John. *The View Over Atlantis*. New York: Ballantine, 1972.

Folklore and Superstition

Coffin, Tristram, and Cohen, Henning, eds. *Folklore in America*. New York: Anchor Books, 1970.

De Lys, Claudia. *A Treasury of American Superstitions*. New York: Philosophical Library, 1948.

Eichler, Lillian. *The Customs of Mankind*. New York: Doubleday, 1924.

Frazer, James. *The Golden Bough*. New York: Macmillan, 1956. (One-volume abridged edition.)

Harley, Rev. Timothy. *Moon Lore*. Rutland, VT: Charles E. Tuttle Co., 1970.

Leach, Maria. *The Soup Stone: The Magic of Familiar Things*. London: Mayflower, 1954.

Leach, Maria, ed. *The Standard Dictionary of Folklore*. New York: Funk and Wagnalls, 1972.

Lawson, John Cuthbert. *Modern Greek Folklore and Ancient Greek Religion*. New Hyde Park, NY: University Books, 1964.

Randolph, Vance. *Ozark Superstitions*. New York: Columbia University Press, 1947.

Waring, Phillipa. *A Dictionary of Omens and Superstitions*. New York: Ballantine, 1979.

Magic

Agrippa, Henry Cornelius. *The Philosophy of Natural Magic*. Secaucus, NJ: University Books, 1974.

Buckland, Raymond. *Practical Candleburning Rituals*. St. Paul, MN: Llewellyn, 1970.

Burland, C. A. *The Magical Arts: A Short History*. New York: Horizon, 1966.

Burriss, Eli Edward. *Taboo, Magic and Spirits*. New York: Macmillan, 1931.

Chappel, Helen. *The Waxing Moon: A Gentle Guide to Magick*. New York: Links, 1974.

Cunningham, Scott. *Magical Herbalism: The Secret Craft of the Wise*. St. Paul, MN: Llewellyn, 1982.

Fortune, Dion. *The Sea Priestess*. London: Aquarian Press, 1957.

Harner, Michael. *The Way of the Shaman*. New York: Bantam, 1982.

Hayes, Carolyn. *Pergemin*. Chicago: Aries Press, 1937.

Howard, Michael. *Candle Burning: Its Occult Significance*. Wellingtonborough (Northhamptonshire): Aquarian Press, 1975.

———. *The Magic of the Runes*. New York: Weiser, 1980.

Howells, William. *The Heathens: Primitive Man and His Religions*. New York: Doubleday, 1956.

Kenyon, Theda. *Witches Still Live*. New York: Washburn, 1928.

Kittredge, George Lyman. *Witchcraft in Old and New England*. New York: Russell and Russell, 1929.

Lea, Henry Charles. *Materials Toward a History of Witchcraft*. New York: Thomas Yosseloff, 1957.

Leland, C. G. *Etruscan Magic and Occult Remedies*. New Hyde Park, NY: University Books, 1963.

Poinsot, M. C. *The Encyclopedia of Occult Sciences*. New York: Tudor, 1968.

Raven. *The Book of Ways*. Escondido, CA: Nemi Enterprises, 1981.

———. *The Book of Ways Volume Two*. Escondido, CA: Nemi Enterprises, 1982.

Schmidt, Phillip. *Superstition and Magic*. Westminster, MD: The Newman Press, 1963.

Scot, Reginald. *Discoverie of Witchcraft*. New York: Dover, 1972.

Singer, Charles. *From Magic to Science*. New York: Dover, 1958.

Spence, Lewis. *Encyclopedia of Occultism*. New York: University Books, 1960.

Thompson, C. J. S. *The Mysteries and Secrets of Magic*. New York: Olympia Press, 1972.

Valiente, Doreen. *Natural Magic*. New York: St. Martin's Press, 1975.

———. *Where Witchcraft Lives*. London: Aquarian Press, 1962.

Worth, Valerie. *The Crone's Book of Words*. St. Paul, MN: Llewellyn, 1971.